· THE ·
FIVE
HAZARDOUS
ATTITUDES

Ways to Win the War Within

RICKY BROWN

AVAIL

to challenge your own attitudes and emerge stronger, this book is your guide. Prepare to be enlightened and inspired!

—Talaat McNeely
Pastor and CEO of His and Her Money

In the information age, wisdom is in scarce supply. In *The Five Hazardous Attitudes*, Brown reveals the wisdom in self-examination and calls us all to Gospel-centered growth rather than self-improvement. It's a must read for those who are tired of getting in the way of what God has for them.

—Justin E. Giboney
AND Campaign

Cover design by Sara Young
Author photo on cover by Andrew van Tilborgh

ISBN: 978-1-962401-45-6   1 2 3 4 5 6 7 8 9 10

Printed in the United States of America

WHAT PEOPLE ARE SAYING ABOUT
THE FIVE HAZARDOUS ATTITUDES

The Five Hazardous Attitudes is an instructional tool that reads like a novel. It offers invaluable insights into negative attitude types that can impede personal and professional growth. This book illuminates the perilous mindsets that threaten success in careers, ministries, relationships, and beyond. It's a refreshing reminder that true success happens in concert with a positive attitude.

—Pastor John K. Jenkins, Sr.
First Baptist Church of Glenarden Maryland

In, *The Five Hazardous Attitudes: Ways to Win the War Within*, Ricky Brown provides an insightful book for navigating and recognizing our attitudes and blind spots we all have in a variety of spaces, including leadership. I highly recommend this book to every leader, worker, counselor, and mentor. This compelling guide will be a valuable resource for years to come.

—Dr. Valencia Wiggins, PhD
Psychologist, Educator, and Speaker

Oftentimes, the events and circumstances in our lives are outside of our control. What we can control during those times, though, is our attitude. In *The Five Hazardous Attitudes*, Ricky Brown demonstrates how our flawed thinking can lead to catastrophic outcomes. He then counters these attitudes with perspectives that allow us to make the most of our situations. For anyone who wishes to put their life on an upward trajectory, *The Five Hazardous Attitudes* is required reading.

—*Dave Ferguson*
Author of B.L.E.S.S. *&* Hero Maker

The only thing that shines brighter than Ricky Brown's smile is his heart to help people achieve their best and his desire to point others to Christ. In *The Five Hazardous Attitudes: Ways to Win the War Within*, every reader is going to be moved by the stories that Ricky shares and the practical ways he helps you overcome the war so many of us have running between our ears. The mind is powerful and what we believe about ourselves can make all the difference. Knowing that God is the provider of all gifts and talents, enjoy this great read and learn from a young man that faced adversity but trusted God and used all his talents to glorify him.

—*Jessica Bettencourt*
Author, Speaker, Business Coach

Ricky Brown's *The Five Hazardous Attitudes* is a game-changer! The book vividly captures the consequences of risky decisions and the misguided belief that "it won't happen to me." This book isn't just a warning; it's a wake-up call. Brown's writing is both impactful and relatable, making it a must-read for anyone on the journey of self-discovery. If you're ready

DEDICATION

*To Amber. For every idea I have, you
respond with overwhelming support. The
biggest idea of all being you and I spending
forever together. All the other ideas get
blurry. Thank you for believing in me,
and giving me Karys. I love you both.*

CONTENTS

INTRODUCTION

PILOTS AREN'T THE ONLY PEOPLE WHO SOMETIMES CRASH.

My life has been a series of attitude adjustments, and I'm willing to bet your life has also. You see, we've all heard the common phrase, "Your attitude determines your altitude", but how have we benefited from it? It's not enough to just know it; we have to respond to the knowledge we gain in order to be successful, in order to realize lasting change, or in order for there to be growth. It's been said that the word enemy can be spelled "in-a-me". When we receive wisdom, but don't conform to it, we have to look within for the reason why. I am an active-duty United States Air Force Veteran, and while serving on active duty I have seen how several people can go through the same exact circumstance and experience it very differently. While I was deployed to

Operation Enduring Freedom at Al Udeid AB Qatar, my squadron was working 14-hour shifts in 120-degree heat. For some, it was unbearable. They hated the assignment and they made sure everyone around them knew it. For others, they made the best of an undesirable situation and pressed on. This isn't only true of those who have served in the Armed Forces. How many times have you noticed the attitudes of co-workers or family members differ greatly while experiencing the same situation, only to lay hold of very different outcomes?

An attitude is defined as a proclivity to behave or act a certain way in response to a given situation. So, an attitude is more than just how we emote, it's how we respond. Why is this important? The Federal Aviation Administration has identified Five Hazardous Attitudes as well as the corresponding antidotes to those attitudes that every pilot must learn before becoming a licensed pilot. Our attitude does indeed determine our altitude. Pilots understand this from a physical perspective and so do passengers. A nose-high attitude is used to initiate a climb (going higher or toward the sky). A nose-low attitude is used to initiate a descent (going lower or toward the ground). I have found that people going through life with "nose-low attitudes" often don't know it. For example, you would think that the physical evidence of a nose-low attitude in an airplane is always obvious to a student pilot, but as a certified flight instructor, I can tell you that isn't always the case. If I had a dollar for every time I find myself saying to a student, "You're in a descent." "Add power!" "Pull up!" If it is possible for a student pilot to fly an airplane with a nose-low attitude and be unaware of it despite all the physical evidence of the horizon and the instruments in front of them shouting, "You're losing altitude!" (or going toward the ground), then it's likely that there are people going through life with a nose-low attitude who don't even know it. Their career is shouting, "Pull up!" Their marriage is shouting, "Pull up!" Their business is shouting, "Pull up!" Why is it that an airline passenger can know immediately that their pilots are climbing based on the attitude change of the aircraft and the sound of engines getting louder, but a student pilot can have an aircraft in a nose-low attitude and not know it when they are the ones behind the controls? It's the same reason that you CANNOT coach a basketball game and play in the game at the same time. It's the same reason your personal trainer knew that you had two more reps when you swore you didn't. You see, when we're in the intensity of a situation, we often don't see ourselves the way we truly are. It's not uncommon for a basketball player to take a "good shot" only to have their coach say the shot was forced once the team gets to the huddle. It's not uncommon at all for a student pilot to force a landing that should have been aborted.

I promise to be positive for the lion's share of this book, but let me be unapologetically clear: Hazardous Attitudes can get a pilot killed. Aircraft accident investigators have found that one of these five Hazardous Attitudes has been involved in almost every plane crash. But Hazardous Attitudes can also stop a business, a partnership, an organization, a career, or even a marriage. This book is for anyone who needs an attitude adjustment and the people who support them. Why? Because pilots aren't the only people who sometimes crash.

Now, you could read this book alone, but it will be infinitely more valuable if you share the premise of this book with someone else who can support you and call out your mess. I teach people how to fly airplanes. My student pilots have someone. Me. In addition to being a flight instructor I am also a pastor, and I have been in ministry 20 years. One of the greatest gifts of the church is community.

Who do you have who can point out the blind spots that you may not be able to see? Ask yourself this question: What if the enemy is "in-a-me"? The Five Hazardous Attitudes is a self-awareness tool that will make the difference in you reaching your potential as a business leader, entrepreneur, pastor, spouse, educator, and the list goes on. The good news is that each Hazardous Attitude has a corresponding antidote. Each is delineated in this book. Are you ready? It's time to start your climb.

Chapter 1

DON'T TELL ME: ANTI-AUTHORITY

THE SITUATION

Every day is just like every day in a town like Porter. It sits on the southern shore of Louisiana where the most exciting things that happen are high school football games, or eating the amazing food that is native to Louisiana, but even the thrill of delicious Cajun cuisine fades after a while for the locals. There isn't any tourism except for the occasional time when relatives come to town for a holiday to eat everything that isn't chained down. It's the kind of town that people drive right through on their way to New

Orleans, Destin, Houston, or any city that has attractions and amenities. The residents of Porter don't really expect people to stop unless they are going to the gas station. Yep, there's only one gas station. It's sort of understood that if you're there it's because either you were born there or you'll be leaving shortly.

Every day is just like every day in the town of Porter, the same way every day is just like every day in the life of Tony Decker. Tony played high school football for Central High and graduated when he was eighteen. That was twenty years ago, and his letterman jacket was starting to fray, and his muscular frame had morphed into a beer bod. He's thirty-eight now and his old "glory stories" have been replaced with new ones of younger, more athletic players, and he and his high school sweetheart unfortunately did not work out. He hasn't been able to find the right gig since he left high school either. Jobs are either too long, too short, too hot, too cold, too little, too much . . . so on and so forth, you get the picture. You see the thing is Tony really doesn't care for "too much" of anything, and if you asked him what would be "just right", he couldn't tell you.

Tony's fortune would have a turn for the best with the arrival of National Petroleum, a new oil rigging company specializing in a safe proprietary method that allows them to drill in a way that greatly reduces hazardous occurrences. Their process was arduous but necessary. Even as a newcomer to the industry, they were first-class in safety protocols. The good news for Tony was that National Petroleum extended him a job offer with a salary twice as much as any of his previous "too" jobs. This would be life-changing for Tony. He was overcome with joy and even ecstatic, which was rare for him. He promised himself that this time would be different. This was Tony's big break. The question was, would he break National Petroleum in the process?

THE STORY

The emergence of National Petroleum had provided more excitement in the town of Porter than it had seen in a long time. Home values increased. There were many infrastructure improvements made to roads and bridges to accommodate the massive trucks entering and exiting town. Jobs would come to Porter because of National, and of course one of these jobs was just landed by Tony Decker. He was hired as a lineman to develop and monitor the safe operation of the new pipelines that National would create. Though it was an entry-level position, it did not pay an entry-level salary by Porter's standards. They took the top spot for places you would want to work immediately, being the highest-paying employer in town. National received applications from as far as seventy-five miles away from people willing to commute, and people from other rural towns around the country willing to relocate to Porter. It was a competitive effort to land a gig at National Petroleum and the company did their due diligence to make sure that they hired workers who would safeguard not only their proprietary methods but also their brand. Or so they thought.

As Tony reported for his first day on the job, he went to the gear dispatch center to don his protective equipment. When he received it, he noticed it had an industrial kind of less-than-new type smell to it. Just when he's decided that this is the way protective equipment is supposed to smell, he hears someone yell his name, "Tony Decker!" When Tony turned around, he saw his high school teammate, Bobby Leighton. Though Bobby was covered in protective gear, Tony could recognize his voice anywhere.

"Bobby!" Tony yelled as he slapped Bobby on the shoulder, "How have you been man?"

"I've been good!" Bobby replied.

"Have you kept up with any of the other guys?" Tony asked.

To that, Bobby replied, "Yeah! Some of the fellas just met at LouLou's for drinks the other night, and we told our fair share of Tony Decker stories!"

To that, Tony said, "Aw man I wasn't that interesting was I?"

"Interesting?" Bobby answered, "Man your battles with coach were epic! You wouldn't take no for an answer! You did whatev . . ." At this moment the shift leader rounded everyone up for crew assignments. Tony and Bobby would be assigned to the same team, just like old times. Their reminiscing would continue later.

Bobby and Tony have an interesting past. Tony had a habit of going rogue on the football team whenever he felt the rules were too strict or too silly. If it meant showing up late or bending the team rules at will, Tony did it. But Bobby always took up for him because of his talent. In a town like Porter, if your high school football glory stories are tarnished, then your whole "legacy" is tarnished. And to Tony, the thought of the possibility of conversation centered around him in an unfavorable way worried him. It was eating away at him that the talk at LouLou's was centered around his shenanigans and not his stats on the field.

Tony decided to pick back up. "So, what do you mean I wouldn't take no for an answer?" Tony asked.

"Well, you know, I just mean if you had an idea of how you felt things should be, you wouldn't let it go," Bobby responded.

"Me?" Tony verified. "Explaining why you are right about something and arguing are two different things." Bobby then had a look on his face as though Tony had clearly gone to high school and played on a football team in some alternate universe. Bobby felt Tony couldn't have been at the same Central High he was. So, Bobby decided to pivot the conversation.

"Oh okay, man. I hear you. But hey, I'll be the one showing you the ropes around here. It's very important that we follow the process exactly how it's written or else . . ."

"Or else what?" Tony interrupted.

"Or else we could destroy a lot of water and land, we could make a lot of people sick, and our company would probably fold, and these high-paying jobs we have would be gone, and this town . . ."

"Okay okay okay, I get it" Tony interrupted. "Just let me know the most important stuff." Tony was almost annoyed by Bobby's insistence that he know and understand the rules that were required to be followed for the position. In the back of Bobby's mind, he felt Tony's indifference was reminiscent of the old Tony he knew. Surely, he had changed. Surely, he had matured after all this time. Or had he? You see, people like Tony, who only want to know the "important stuff", have a habit of not knowing the important stuff when they need to know it. Why? Because context is everything and that's what Bobby was desperately trying to convey to Tony. The context of why National's methods matter and are required by the Federal Energy Regulatory Commission. The context of the safety hazards to the land and the water. The context of what this company means to the town of Porter. Without the context, the important stuff can seem not so important. Tony and Bobby seemed to be picking up right where they left off with Bobby showing Tony the rules and Tony seeming completely disinterested. But to better understand Tony's past, we need to go back to his childhood. Back when he was creating habits around authority.

BE RIGHT BACK

Porter was the kind of place where fairytales happened as they pertained to love. If you locked eyes with a girl while at recess in elementary school, it wasn't far-fetched to think that you might end up marrying her one day. This was the case with Tony's parents, Bill Decker and Amy Farmer. They were in the same class in the 5th grade and ended up in the same homeroom in middle school. They officially began dating in high school and got married the Saturday after graduation. Shortly after that, Tony was born. Bill and Amy had fallen in love too fast, too hard, and too young. The happy times were as high as the heavens. The sad times felt like being plummeted into the lower depths of the earth. Their relationship was a rollercoaster filled with thrills, dips, bends, and scares. When they were hot, they were on fire. When they weren't, they were as cold as ice. Though they were both from Porter, they came from very different families. Bill was a product of hardworking parents with a strongly formed culture and belief system, and they really didn't see the need for any type of religion. His dad held the wheel of the family ship with a very tight grip. He felt it was his and his alone to direct, and he would never let it go under any circumstance. As a result, Bill ended up being more of an emperor than a father. Even though he was never close to his dad, he admired him and wanted to be like him. Amy came from a home of people who would consider themselves "spiritual", but her mother was the primary leader in the home. She spent her childhood years watching her dad stay out of her mom's way which is the converse of what Bill witnessed as a boy in his home.

Bill and Amy's family-of-origin issues eventually metastasized, as they never received the care of counseling or invested in their marriage. For Bill, marriage began to feel like more of a prison sentence than it did something that was the source of great joy. In his mind, he tried to take the lead and guide his home to calmer shores, but that was the opposite of what Amy experienced as a child so she often felt intruded upon when Bill would assert himself as the leader of the family. Bill would become increasingly more absent, and he would often find a place to wander. They began to argue for breakfast, lunch, and dinner. Tony also noticed they started disregarding agreed-upon family staples such as meals together, family time, and church on Sundays.

Tony's attitude and emotional health took an obvious decline as well. He didn't feel any closer to his dad than Bill felt to his. The fact that the people who were responsible for Tony were not being very good leaders began to inform his thoughts about authority. Bill and Amy both constantly said one thing and did another. The one thing that affected Tony the most was how they said they loved each other but he witnessed very few acts of love in how they spoke to each other, treated each other, and the lack of care they had for each other. It wasn't that he was upset at them for having problems. Even at a young age, he understood that tough times are sometimes inevitable. What he couldn't seem to get around was how they were choosing to navigate their tough times. After all, everyone knows that a person piloting a ship should try to avoid the rocks and not willingly crash into them. It created trust issues that would need to be resolved before he could have a healthy view of authority. Tony felt someone shouldn't be telling him what to do who doesn't do it themselves. So, in Tony's mind, he questioned why he should submit to authority when authority could be wrong.

Bill and Amy's differences left unattended eventually proved to be too much. One day when Tony was only eight years old, Bill went out for cigarettes and never came back. Every prized possession that Bill had vanished. He had packed and he was gone. Amy knew that things were rough between them, but she didn't expect that he would "go out for cigarettes". She often wondered, if her family had been more like Bill's, would he have stayed? Tony never heard from him or saw him again. The last words that Bill said to Tony pierce almost every moment of silence that Tony can manage to grasp, "Be right back." The final words to Tony from the most important authority figure in his life were a lie. This very unfortunate circumstance shaped some deeply held beliefs inside of Tony around authority. Many of which were unhealthy. Tony would grow up questioning or disregarding authority at every phase of his life. Tony's Hazardous Attitude of Anti-Authority became rooted in his disdain for his parents. Mostly his dad. Because in his heart, he felt that, at a minimum, his dad should have either said goodbye, or at least come back home from the store.

SCHOOL DAYS

As the bell rang at Central High late one Friday afternoon, it signaled to every student that they could now be free from the "tyranny" of the system of formal education and all its structure for one more weekend. At least for everyone except the football team. They had a game that night and as always, Coach had given them strict instructions to not leave the campus. The program provided everything they needed. Porter was a town that invested heavily in high school football with a "spare no expense" approach to the program, shown especially in how they built the athletic field house. It had plush locker rooms, a lounge, a smoothie bar for protein shakes, an Olympic-sized pool, cryo-freeze tanks, and sleep rooms for kids who may have played too much Playstation the night before a game. It was a mini-NFL-like facility. All their game day food was catered in and there was absolutely no reason whatsoever to leave their majestic field house, but as you may have guessed, Tony found one.

Tony was very nervous about the game because he had some not-so-great plays in the previous two games, and he was starting to let it get into his head. Remember, in Porter, if your football glory stories are tarnished, your whole legacy is tarnished. Tony didn't have much vision for what would be next after high school so as far as he was concerned—this was it. This was everything. Tony decided to leave campus against the coach's direction. The other guys on the team were being a little rambunctious and he felt like he wanted to get to a place of solitude. So, to Tony, this justified breaking the silly rules. The only problem was Tony had a habit of disregarding authority and Coach was getting tired of it. As Tony tried to sneak his way back into the field house, he heard a car door shut behind him. When he turned around, he saw his coach getting a book out of his car and staring at him like he wanted to choke him. He was busted.

"Tony, are you kidding me!" Coach shouted. "If there was one player I had to bet money on who couldn't stay on campus on game day, it would be you and I would be rich!" Tony didn't particularly like being told that betting against his ability to follow the rules would make his coach a winner. He didn't care for the volume of his voice either. Never mind the fact that the reason this confrontation was happening in the first place was because Tony didn't care for the game-day rule.

"I couldn't just sit here all night waiting for the game, Coach. I needed to get out of here." Tony explained.

"Everyone else is able to do it! Why can't you!" Coach screamed. Now it was at this point that this situation was going to go either one of two ways: Coach was going to bench Tony for breaking the game day rule and his lack of taking responsibility, or Tony was going to have to quickly realize the error of his ways, take ownership, and get back in the good favor of his coach. Yep, Tony chose option Λ.

Tony then shouted, "Because it's a stupid rule! And I think it's silly that we can't go anywhere on game day!"

Now let's review. Tony just told Coach that his rule was stupid, which could also infer that Tony thinks the rule-maker is stupid, which in this case would be Coach. The commotion was so loud it penetrated the expensive field house walls, so Bobby Leighton poked his head outside of the field house door to see what all the fuss was about. By then, Coach had some time to compose himself and regain control of the situation. He paused, gathered his thoughts, garnered his breath, and then almost like a judge, rendered his verdict, "Tony you have a problem with authority. When you think rules are silly and unnecessary you break them, and I would be setting a terrible example by allowing you to play tonight. I'm sitting you down." Both Tony and Bobby's eyes were wide open, and they both seemed to have forgotten to breathe. They couldn't believe it.

Here's why. Tony played defensive back commonly known as "DB". The DB's job in football is to either prevent the opponents from catching the ball or stop the yardage gain by tackling the offensive player with the ball. Tony put his heart and soul into every hit. It was his way of hitting back at the life that he felt had hit him so many times. If you dared to catch the ball on his side of the field, he would absolutely rock you. Tony was a "lights out" kind of DB. Central absolutely needed Tony to win that night or else they could risk falling behind and not making the playoffs. Tony's Hazardous Attitude of Anti-Authority was hurting everyone, not just himself. Bobby looked as though he wanted to try to appeal on Tony's behalf. To that, Coach responded with a look that said, "Don't even think about it." Was stepping out once for some fresh air against the rules such a terrible thing? No. But Coach had just become tired of the habitual disregard for his position that had become Tony's mantra. Did Coach want to hurt the team or even Tony? Absolutely not. But he realized that in leadership, small corrections like benching someone could help avoid an even greater correction in his future. The only question was whether Tony would ever adhere to small corrections or if there would be a big correction in his future. Only time would tell.

BACK TO THE RIG

The executive team at National Petroleum was beyond thrilled when the Federal Energy Regulatory Commission approved their proprietary methods. But it was not without a mountain of stipulations, one of which mandated strict adherence to monitoring and reporting. National deployed a cadre of specialized equipment used to monitor pressure levels and flow data in real-time to avoid any mishap by catching it before it happened. The precision of the data they processed was within a pen dot of accuracy as long as the workers followed the required procedures. Bobby had the task of teaching National's OMH Protocols to Tony. This was not an art; it was a science. They knew exactly what was optimal, marginal, and hazardous (OMH). If the flow data was optimal, no problem—full steam ahead. If the ratings were marginal, it meant that something would need adjusting before it escalated to hazardous. Part of the mandate required National line workers to keep a paper log for the first three years of operation. Sure, their multi-million-dollar system recorded and analyzed data. But software could fail. Hardware could fail. Computer systems could fail, and the best method of prevention was the added human policing of system performance. It was the only way this operation would be foolproof. The requirement of meticulous human scanning was also the only way National was given the green light by FERC. Bobby and

Tony had donned their protective gear, they trained on the safety protocols at length for several days, and they were now ready to work. What could go wrong?

Tony and Bobby had been working together for a month and the processes were starting to get to a level of automaticity that was becoming natural. But they were also becoming monotonous and boring to Tony. He was being compensated very well for the work he was doing, but he couldn't manage to see all of the monitoring as necessary. Bobby noticed that whenever it was Tony's turn to monitor, he skipped lines in the log, wasn't paying much attention, and seemed disinterested in the procedures. Blank lines in the logs that National was required to maintain would mean an immediate suspension of their business in the event there was an unannounced audit. Strict adherence to the monitoring provisions set forth by the Federal Energy Regulatory Commission was a hard standard. The only way to prove you are monitoring is to actually monitor, and blank logs would mean a hard stop for National.

"Hey man, are you good?" Bobby inquired.

"Yeah, why wouldn't I be?" answered Tony.

"You seem distracted."

"Well I mean, we've been doing this for hours. . . . what time is our break?"

At this, Bobby attempted to intervene with Tony and his case of apathy. "Hey man, I get that the hours are long but we have a job to do, and you haven't been accomplishing all of the lines on the log. Have you even been doing the checks?" It was at this moment that Tony's face filled with blood. He was furious that Bobby would question his work ethic and as far as Tony was concerned, his integrity.

"Don't you think I know what we need to be doing by now!" Tony screamed. "We have been doing the same thing for a month over and over again and nothing ever changes!"

To that, Bobby interjected, "Hey man I get that each day is pretty standard but . . ."

"But what?!" Tony challenged. "This isn't even necessary! In fact, I think it's stupid that we have to write down every single friggin' thing that this system does!"

"But Tony, you know that this rule is a provision that must be honored in order for us to do this work in the first place." Bobby reasoned.

"Well, I think it's silly that we have to jot down every single measurement like we are a bunch of space suit secretaries or something! This is just dumb!"

It was at this moment that Bobby knew who the person in front of him really was. This was Tony Decker. Class skipping Tony. Football practice skipping Tony. Rule-breaking, bull-headed, authority-bucking Tony. Bobby began to wonder how he would handle this situation. If it were just one outburst on a bad day from Tony, that would have been one thing. But the man in front of him was still the boy beside him from high school. Bobby decided to talk to the supervisor in charge and to his surprise, he wasn't met with open arms or even a little understanding for that matter. His supervisor simply told him that, from his perspective, half the guys on the crew had a bad attitude and that if he got rid of them all, they wouldn't have any employees. Bobby shared with the supervisor that he didn't understand. Tony's attitude wasn't just bad, it was hazardous. Something detrimental and monumental was bound to happen with Tony on the job site. He disagreed and they ended the discussion.

Three months after their last blow-up, Tony seemed to be doing fine on the job. In fact, it wasn't uncommon for Tony to hold the line while Bobby ate lunch or went to the restroom. Sure, Tony seemed just as disinterested in FERC's monitoring provisions as before, but at least he was accomplishing them, or so it seemed. Bobby had begun to trust Tony more as well. He didn't like treating him like he was a child and he felt that Tony needed responsibility. So, inch by inch, Bobby began to allow Tony to assume more of a leadership role with their supervisor's approval. What Bobby didn't understand was that this was not what Tony needed after all. Because the one thing you don't want to give someone with a Hazardous Attitude of Anti-Authority is authority.

There's a saying that if you give some people an inch, they'll become a cowboy. Tony might as well have worn a shirt that said, "Getty up!" The reason Tony was able to accomplish the monitoring logs so consistently was because he wasn't actually taking the time to read the pressure and flow measurements. He just decided that they were always within a certain range, and he was tired of doing it because it was silly, so he would just keep the numbers that he recorded in the ballpark and everyone would be happy. Or so he thought. Not having actual measurements for the pressure and flow of the lines would prove to cause huge problems. There were National engineers depending on the logs to make adjustments and if the numbers were phony, which they were, then the adjustments to the system would be off—which they were.

Bobby had taken a day and a half of leave to take his wife to several doctor's appointments. It was about one in the afternoon when he was starting his shift. As Bobby exited the gear dispatch center, he heard the system warning siren and began to sprint to his workstation. Tony had been in charge for the last day and a half. To his surprise, Tony did not seem overly excited or concerned. The first step in the protocol for a warning system siren was to cycle the pressure valves and make positive contact with the engineering team. "Have you cycled? Have you made contact?" Bobby asked.

"No, because I'm sure it will be fine," Tony responded.

"Tony! Are there any rules you don't find pointless?" Bobby decided that a lesson for Tony in self-awareness would have to wait. He was a one-man show at this point and he needed to get started on the emergency checklist because the siren wasn't stopping. As Bobby tried to maneuver the pressure relief valve he noticed it felt stuck but decided to continue. In his mind, it was better to risk the worst-case scenario because he didn't know how much time the system had before it would erupt. He knew Tony had wasted precious seconds by not following the procedure. Bobby understood the risk but with the haunting of the siren, he decided to try one more time, and that's when it happened. The pressure relief valve exploded and hit Bobby in the head. With a palpitating heart, Tony finally sprung into action and began providing aid for Bobby.

"Hang on buddy, I got you—I promise I got you!" Tony assured.

"Move back! Give him some room!" The emergency personnel said as they arrived on the scene.

After what felt like an eternity, Bobby was airlifted from the sight to the local hospital where he was admitted into the ICU.

Bobby suffered a traumatic brain injury (TBI) and unfortunately would never be the same. Some of his motor skills needed for basic daily living activities were significantly diminished to the point that he would now need long-term care. Tony was fired, of course, and so was their supervisor for his lack of leadership. It took Tony more than a year to find a new job which gave him a lot of time to think. Not only about the incident but also about what led to it. Tony was very introspective for the first time in his life. The last thing he wanted was to hurt anyone. Especially not someone like Bobby who had always looked out for his best interest. There was something deep down inside of Tony that was beginning to connect the dots. The childhood dot was now connecting to the high school football team dot to the National Petroleum dot. Tony also lost a lot that day. He lost a friendship that can never be replaced, and a great-paying career with benefits and retirement. One with a salary he would never attain again. Bobby was thankful to be alive and Tony learned a lot about himself that he would rely on moving forward. Tony's biggest takeaway from the situation was that a Hazardous Attitude of Anti-Authority not only impacts the person with the Hazardous Attitude— but everyone around them.

Anti-authority—"Don't tell me."

Antidote —Say it out loud: "Follow the rules; they're usually right."

Plainly put, Anti-Authority is the Hazardous Attitude found in people who don't like anyone telling them what to do. They have a tendency to view rules as silly, unnecessary, or overkill. There is a myriad of reasons why this may be. Maybe they were allowed to do as they pleased as children. In the household they grew up in, they were allowed by their parents to kick and scream on the floor of a supermarket in protest for not buying them ice cream. But the most common reason is unresolved trauma. Now let me say that I absolutely give room for humanness. People in authority can sometimes give instructions that are harmful or lack a tangible benefit. There are appropriate times to question the rules. There are appropriate times to verify and even re-verify.

I was once given some instructions by an airport worker that did not sit right with me. In my gut, I knew something was off. I second-guessed it. So, I asked for clarity. I was glad I did because his mistake could have cost me my life. I will never forget it. But if the natural inclination of a person is to question, rebuff, or even in some cases ignore instructions, they have a Hazardous Attitude of Anti-Authority. Did you know there are highways in the sky? Absolutely! Pilots have to abide by certain speed restrictions, altitude restrictions, and direction restrictions, or else air travel would be total chaos. Could you imagine if every pilot challenged the authority and guidelines of the highways in the air? Planes would literally be falling out of the sky left and right. There's something dangerous that happens with people who have an anti-authority attitude. When the attitude surfaces in them and nothing catastrophic happens, the attitude grows and when it resurfaces, the next time it will be bigger and stronger than before. This is the calamity of anti-authority; it's like a snowballing debt with a balloon note right at the end with no notice that it has become due. The cost is always higher than anyone can afford to pay. Let's review some key moments in Tony's story to help us gain a better understanding.

ATTITUDE ADJUSTMENTS:

1) **Tony's jobs are usually "too".**

He hasn't been able to find the right gig since he left high school either. Jobs are either too long, too short, too hot, too cold, too little, too much . . . so on and so forth, you get the picture. You see the thing is Tony really doesn't care for "too much" of anything, and if you asked him what would be "just right", he couldn't tell you.

Even when Tony was compensated far above anything he ever had, it still did not motivate him to submit to authority. If people have a Hazardous Attitude of

Anti-Authority, paying them more will only make them a higher-earning insubordinate. Remember, the mindset isn't "I don't get paid enough for this." The mindset is, "These rules are silly and unnecessary." So paying them more will likely only temporarily delay the inevitable, at best. Have you found yourself in a place where you feel as though you aren't compensated enough for what you do? Be honest enough with yourself to admit it if the problem is your attitude.

2) I wasn't that interesting, was I?

"Yeah! Some of the fellas just met at LouLou's for drinks the other night, and we told our fair share of Tony Decker stories!"

To that, Tony said, "Aw man I wasn't that interesting was I?"

"Interesting?" Bobby answered, "Man your battles with coach were epic! You wouldn't take no for an answer!"

People who have a Hazardous Attitude of Anti-Authority are often the talk of the town, and everyone knows it but them. They need people to help them see themselves. If not, they never will. The question is, will you listen when they speak?

3) Higher stakes won't do it.

"Oh okay, man. I hear you. But hey, I'll be the one showing you the ropes around here. It's very important that we follow the process exactly how it's written or else . . ."

"Or else what?" Tony interrupted.

"Or else we could destroy a lot of water and land, we could make a lot of people sick, and our company would probably fold, and these high-paying jobs we have would be gone, and this town . . ."

"Okay okay okay, I get it" Tony interrupted. "Just let me know the most important stuff." Tony was almost annoyed by Bobby's insistence that he know and understand the rules that were required to be followed for the position.

Even when Tony is made to understand that the stakes are higher than they have ever been for Porter, he still didn't change his attitude. Shouting at a person with a Hazardous Attitude so that they understand the seriousness nature of a situation is fruitless. What needs to change is not their assessing ability, it's their level of self-awareness.

4) What lies beneath.

The fact that the people who were responsible for Tony were not being very good leaders began to inform his thoughts about authority. Bill and Amy both constantly said one thing and did another.

Hazardous Attitudes are usually the fruit of unresolved trauma. At the crucial moment in Tony's life when he was forming his beliefs about authority, the ones who had charge over him fumbled miserably. Not because they divorced, but because they were hypocritical. Again, in Tony's mind, why wouldn't his parents try to avoid the rocks? From his perception, they seemed to steer right into them in order to injure each other. The problem was that impressionable Tony was on board the family ship as well. The worst thing his dad could have done was to tell Tony he was coming back and never return. How might you be justifying disregarding authority based on past traumatic experiences?

5) I had a good reason.

"I couldn't just sit here all night waiting for the game, Coach. I needed to get out of here." Tony explained.

"Everyone else is able to do it! Why can't you!"
Coach screamed.

It's not that people with a Hazardous Attitude of Anti-Authority don't think. They do. They think there is a sufficient reason to break the rules. If a rule or provision stands in opposition to what they want, they will see the rule or provision as silly compared to their desired outcome. And something so silly as a rule shouldn't keep them from what they think is best, right? What might you be labeling as frivolous that could actually have substantial long-term implications?

6) Repetition is purgatory.

"Hey man, are you good?" Bobby inquired.

"Yeah, why wouldn't I be?" answered Tony.

"You seem distracted."

"Well I mean, we've been doing this for hours. . . . what time is our break?"

At this, Bobby attempted to intervene with Tony and his case of apathy. "Hey man, I get that the hours are long but we have a job to do, and you haven't been accomplishing all of the lines on the log. Have you even been doing the checks?" It was at this moment that Tony's face filled with blood. He was furious that Bobby would question his work ethic and as far as Tony was concerned, his integrity.

To someone who has a Hazardous Attitude of Anti-Authority, doing what is demanded over and over again is like putting your money in bags with holes. It's like asking a cat to refrain from chasing the mouse. It's in its nature. That's what cats do; they chase things. To place someone with a Hazardous Attitude of Anti-Authority in a role where they have to do the opposite of what they think they should be doing multiple times a day is purgatory. From their perspective, you just told them to go to hell. It's not that they don't want to follow the rules; they can't until they have had an attitude adjustment. Here's my advice to you: If you're in a role that requires you to do the same thing over and over again, and you hate that thing, quit. Find something else to do that allows you to be free and spontaneous. Tony could have saved his friend from having a TBI if he had done so. In fact, if this is you, your co-workers are likely waiting on you to quit.

7) Hazardous Attitudes compound like interest.

It was at this moment that Bobby knew who the person in front of him really was. This was

Tony Decker. Class skipping Tony. Football practice skipping Tony. Rule-breaking, bull-headed, authority-bucking Tony. Bobby began to wonder how he would handle this situation. If it were just one outburst on a bad day from Tony, that would have been one thing. But the man in front of him was still the boy beside him from high school.

If people with Hazardous Attitudes do not have an awakening, it will eventually compound into a great catastrophe as in the case of Tony Decker.

8) The Hazardous Attitude of Anti-Authority always comes with the highest cost.

Bobby suffered a traumatic brain injury and unfortunately would never be the same. Some of his motor skills needed for basic daily living activities were significantly diminished to the point that he would now need long-term care. . . . Tony also lost a lot that day. He lost a friendship that can never be replaced, and a great-paying career with benefits and retirement. One with a salary he would never attain again.

This is the reason intervention is paramount. The cost is simply too high. Irreversible damage is done when Anti-Authority is fully grown.

Chapter 2

IT WON'T HAPPEN TO ME: INVULNERABILITY

I f people never acted as though they were invulnerable, we would have little need for a criminal justice system. The number of people who commit crimes caring nothing about the consequence are small in number. I admit that there are people in our society who are not deterred even the least bit by greater penalties, but they are not the norm.

I've done over seven years of prison ministry, preaching, and teaching in both state and federal correctional facilities. It's something I absolutely love to do. We have seen so many lives transformed. On the one hand, some people who have not gone to prison feel as though inmates have made their choice in life and that I should spend my time elsewhere with people who have not gone down that same path. I understand their sentiment, though I disagree. On the other hand, there are many people who are cerebrally unavailable until they are in prison. Meaning, they are not in a head space to hear and understand until the weight of justice rests squarely on their own shoulders. They simply have their head full of other thoughts, one of which is not, "What if I get caught?" What I have found is the one thing that most people serving time in prison have in common is a mindset that says, "Yes people get caught and are convicted of crimes and sent to prison, but it won't happen to me." This is the Hazardous Attitude of Invulnerability. This was the attitude of Eddie and Jessika Esposito.

THE DON

If you had ten men in a line-up and were tasked with choosing the one you thought would be the most successful solely on their appearance, rhetorical skill, charisma, mannerisms, and posturing, you would absolutely choose Eddie Esposito. Eddie oozed confidence and competence. He was full of life and energy and had about a teaspoon of too much ego. His general disposition was that luck was on his side and that some way, somehow, things would always work out in his favor, even if the "things" in question were not quite legal. He's the kinda guy that seems to always stumble upon secret information about "the next big thing". As though somehow there was a monopoly on information. He doesn't see this as a potential liability or character flaw. After all, luck is on his side, right? Some of the people around him challenged his business dealings, but most enabled him, his wife Jessika included. After all, Eddie did have some wins under his belt. He was innovative enough to see that people would order more food if the wait for delivery wasn't as long. He started a courier service that utilized college kids on bicycles long before the days of DoorDash. Eddie was an enterprising entrepreneur with all the tools to "make it big". If he were a shooting guard in the game of basketball, you could say that the rim looked like the size of the ocean in his eyes. To Eddie, he just couldn't miss.

But he suffered from something called, "just one more". His insatiable desire to succeed was made malignant by his need to impress his family, and it would eventually create a perfect storm. Eddie came from a strong Italian family of immigrants who were successful businesspeople. The unspoken proverb of his family seemed to be, "As a man earns, so is he." Though it was never articulated explicitly, Eddie always felt like his self-worth was inextricably bound to his net worth. And this only fed his desire for more. His constant meditation was all about one more deal, one more idea, and even just one more scheme. Eddie had a bad case of the "can't help its" and Jessika wasn't about to rain on his parade. She believed in Eddie but unfortunately to a fault. Culturally it would be out of place to challenge his integrity or intelligence, but someone needed to. Jessika was absolutely the only person breathing that Eddie might listen to. Jessika had Eddie's attention. She had his heart. She had his trust. She had his respect. But what she didn't have at times was the nerve to stand up to him. If you think I am saying that Eddie needed a handler, then you would be correct.

Confidence is absolutely essential in everything we do. But the question is . . . confidence in what?

That's what we do when we see a child reaching for something that is hot as though they are invulnerable to burns; we handle them and remove them from the situation. The obvious problem is that Eddie is not a child, he's an adult. He's not Jessika's dependent; he's her husband. Keep in mind that Eddie isn't dumb, by any means. In fact, he's brilliant. Eddie's problem is that deep down inside he believes that no matter what, he can't lose and that consequences are real but they'll never apply to him because, after all, luck is on his side—or so he thinks. Jessika's problem is that she believes that he's correct. But what about confidence? Confidence is absolutely essential in everything we do. But the question is . . . confidence in what? If a person's confidence is in the fact that they have taken the time to prepare, research, study, and develop a sound strategy for whatever task is before them, then great. If they have done their homework, then they should be confident! But if a person's confidence is in luck, chance, or mere karma, then that isn't confidence—that's being foolish. Invulnerability is the Hazardous Attitude that produces a behavior rooted in the belief, "it won't happen to me."

THE MEET UP

On a frigid New Jersey morning at 7:38 a.m., Eddie stepped outside of his house to get his newspaper and let the dog out. Jessika was still half asleep, but she could hear their German Shepherd greeting the other dogs on their street. Eddie saw a dark-colored car parked on his street a few houses down that he didn't recognize. He couldn't see into the car to see if anyone was inside, but he really didn't think anything of it. Eddie stared at the car for a bit, but it was cold outside, and his dog was doing everything he could to make eye contact with him to let him know he was finished doing his business. As Eddie turned to go back into the house, he noticed that one of his neighbors was on the porch gazing at him, not really prepared to wave or acknowledge that he was being awkward. Eddie then sorta grunted to himself, turned to open the door, and braced himself in the door frame as his dog charged into the house to escape the cold air.

"What were you doing?" Jessika asked.

"I had to let the dog out while I was getting the paper and I saw a car at the end of the street," Eddie responded.

"Yeah, so? What's the deal with the car?" Jessika asked.

"I don't know, babe, it's just a car. We gotta get going or we'll be late."

Jessica and Eddie were on their way to a very important business meeting that could be monumental for their enterprise. They were a bit concerned about partnering with this particular individual because the word on the street was that he had some less-than-integral business dealings in the past. They understood that the company you keep will foretell either your rise or your demise, but to Eddie and Jessika, the benefits always far outweighed the risks. This deal would mean a lot of money—I mean A LOT of money—and if they played this right, this could be the cornerstone deal on which their empire rested. It was customary for Eddie to bring Jessika along to business meetings. As charming and persuasive as Eddie was, Jessika was absolutely mesmerizing when given an audience. They were an irresistible combo. She saw things that he didn't see at times. Sometimes when deals were about to fall through, she would step in and sweeten the pot. Not to mention the times when the vision the men around Eddie had was too small, Jessika would point them to a bigger picture with an even bigger payout. She did this with ease. Her biggest challenge would be to help Eddie see that invulnerability is a luxury that no one owns because it's a luxury that no one can afford.

> ## The company you keep will foretell either your rise or your demise.

As they pulled into the parking lot of the very luxe office building where their meeting would be held, Eddie leaned over and kissed Jessika on her left cheek and said, "This is it, babe. This is what we've been working for. You'll see this time, I promise."

"I trust you, Eddie." Jessika affirmed. "You've been on a roll!"

With that, they exited the car and headed upstairs to meet with D'Angelo Romano, a person with almost as much charisma as Eddie but with an extensive criminal record, and an even longer list of lawyers on his payroll. Eddie was not a novice entrepreneur, but as far as criminal enterprise was concerned, Eddie was a little porch pup and D'Angelo was a huge junkyard dog with a big bark and even bigger bite, if you know what I mean.

"Eddie! Welcome, my friend! And this very lovely lady must be your wife, I presume?" D'Angelo started.

"Thank you, my friend. Yes, this is my wife, Jessika." Eddie responded thinking to himself that D'Angelo did not need to put "very" in front of lovely and that his use of the word was unnecessary.

"Let's sit down and talk business. You've brought quite the beauty with you so we're already moving in the right direction," D'Angelo mentioned. Jessika rolled her eyes knowing that her greatest asset was her business acumen and not her looks, but she was willing to put up with it momentarily for Eddie's sake.

"Eddie, I am going to make you an offer you can't refuse. I am looking to expand my humble empire I have been building in the auto sales industry. We secure our inventory, finance the cars, insure the cars, and we also do all the title work in-house as well. No one else has any involvement in any part of the process. I'd like you to run our next location as a part owner." D'Angelo offered. Eddie then had a look of confusion on his face that suggested he wasn't exactly blown away by D'Angelo's presentation. Eddie was a "swing for the fence" kinda guy, and this sounded like barely getting on first base to him. Was D'Angelo offering him a job? If so, Eddie wasn't interested.

Eddie looked at Jessika to gauge her reaction and then said, "What's so great and irresistible about that D'Angelo? I'm not exactly ready to walk down the aisle here if you know what I mean."

"I'll tell you what's so great about it. I am offering you the opportunity to take 50 percent, which is something I absolutely never do."

"I don't get it," Eddie challenged. "Why would you front the money for a new location, allow me to be part owner, and then allow me to take half? Doesn't make sense, pal."

At this point Jessika was proud of Eddie's clarifying questions. Neither of them was a pushover and she liked that he wasn't falling for the proverbial "banana in the tailpipe."

"Well, Eddie." D'Angelo replied. "I will need you to make a few adjustments as needed along the way to make sure everything balances out. But not to worry, my umbrella company runs every facet of the operation from title to insurance to sales. So, no one will ever be the wiser. This will mean a lot of money for you two. You will not regret it."

"So what's the big takeaway here, D'Angelo?" Eddie asked. "Why us and how much money are we talking?"

"I need new faces for this next location." D'Angelo explained. "Let's just say the usual suspects are becoming too familiar to watchful eyes and I really need a fresh look."

At this point, Eddie didn't like D'Angelo's lack of just spitting it out and speaking plainly. His speech was extremely veiled and neither Eddie nor Jessika liked it at this point. They felt as though D'Angelo didn't take them as the real deal. "Look, I need to know right now how or why this may make a lot of money for us because the used car market isn't exactly blazing hot right now, if you know what I mean?" Eddie challenged.

"Fine. I can see that the two of you aren't much for mystery. I need another way to legitimize cash flow," D'Angelo answered.

"You want us to clean money?" Eddie inquired.

"I want you to run the location while my people clean the money. I just need two nice-looking, upstanding citizens such as yourselves who have high-volume sales experience in order to make this work. The more you sell, the more we clean. Bada bing, bada boom."

What D'Angelo was describing was money laundering. The act of taking money that was gained through illegal transactions and filtering it through legitimate businesses to make it look like the original source of the funds came from a business that was legal. Eddie and Jessika looked at each other as if to say they were not impressed. Beyond their lack of enthusiasm, there was something in their gut telling them that this might cost them more trouble than they could afford. But they felt as though they couldn't walk away without knowing a figure of how much money this could mean for them.

At this point, because of the looks on their faces, D'Angelo begins to preemptively rebut. "How about this, help me get this new location up and running, let me take care of the rinse and repeat, and if in three months you're not averaging 100k a month between the sales and your cut for what you're doing for me, I'll buy you out."

"100,000 dollars a month!?" Eddie immediately looked at Jessika with puppy dog eyes as if to say he had fallen hopelessly in love. Not with her or D'Angelo, but with the idea of making more money in a month than he had made in almost a year. To Eddie, there was nothing more romantic than money—not even Jessika. Eddie quaked and trembled like an addict. He had heard all that he needed to hear. But Jessika didn't seem nearly as intoxicated as Eddie.

"Wow. That's really something," Jessica commented.

"Something, babe? This is it. This is the deal we've been waiting on and there's no way we can fail!" Eddie tried to convince her.

"Well, there is one way," Jessica mentioned.

"Yeah, what way is that?" Eddie asked.

"What if we get caught? What if this doesn't go as planned and the new faces become the old ones, Eddie?"

"That's not gonna happen," Eddie assured. "Right, D'Angelo?"

This was now a defining moment in this conversation and D'Angelo would have to step up to the podium of their hearts and minds and give his best address. Eddie was salivating, but Jessika? Not so much. The deciding factor as to whether this partnership would form would be if they would eventually go to jail. D'Angelo would just have to convince them that they would never get caught. And Eddie didn't believe getting caught was possible for him in the first place.

D'Angelo cleared his throat and began to speak. "I've never once had anyone in my organization serve prison time. Not once. And as sharp as you are, we ain't going to start with you two."

Well, this was all Eddie needed to hear. Unfortunately, it was the speech that Jessika needed to hear to go from undecided to all-in. Here is an unshakeable truth: Just because you haven't been caught doesn't mean you never will. D'Angelo, with almost surgeon-like precision, cut subcutaneously through all of Eddie's layers and managed to put his finger right on the place in Eddie's soul that needed to be repaired but instead, he damaged it further. It's the place that housed his belief that he is invulnerable, and consequences won't happen to him. With that, Eddie stood up, they shook hands and departed.

Here is an unshakeable truth: Just because you haven't been caught doesn't mean you never will.

AND THEY'RE OFF

The next few months would be integral for this new operation. Eddie and Jessika knew nothing about the used car business, but they knew what they liked and didn't like about the cars they had purchased in the past, and the sales part wasn't going to be an issue at all. These two had the ability to sell a drowning man a glass of water! They began to have the inventory pour in and they were getting rid of it pretty quickly. D'Angelo's crew was washing more money than Eddie and Jessika could have ever dreamed of. It was almost euphoric. It was as if they were dreaming. It just seemed unreal how much money was passing through their operation. But if something seems too good to be true, it's because it usually is. D'Angelo was laundering so much money through Eddie's dealership that Eddie had to roll back the odometers on the cars so he could sell them at a higher price and create more margin. Eddie never asked what kind of business dealings D'Angelo was into or where the money they were cleaning came from. He was willfully ignorant. He just saw this as an opportunity of a lifetime to develop a war chest of cash to do the other things in business that he really wanted to do that required more liquid capital. To Eddie, this was the cornerstone deal on which their empire would rest. This was the seed that would change the trajectory of their family for generations to come . . . or was it? In Eddie's mind, because he was a good guy, and good things happen to good people, he just could never accept that bad deeds also have bad consequences for the person who does them.

"Do you think we're in over our heads?" Jessika cautioned.

"Yeah, I do. I think we're over our heads in cash—what are you talking about, babe?" Eddie responded.

"I mean things seem to be going fine but we're taking risks with cleaning dirty money and rolling back odometers like this is a video game and we have three lives, Eddie."

"Forgive me but I'm not seeing your point, Jessika!"

"The point is, Eddie, that we don't have three lives because God only gave us one life and I don't want to spend the rest of it in jail, you moron!"

"You knew what you were getting into, and besides, no one in his organization has ever done time and that won't start with us!"

At this point, it was clear that there was trouble in paradise. They were starting to be bolder in their illegal business affairs. They were rolling back the odometers by larger numbers. They were cleaning money in higher and higher amounts to the point that they didn't care about the ines-capable fact that the greedier you get, the more people watch you eat. And people were watching. And when I say people, I mean the Federal Bureau of Investigation.

HERE WE GROW AGAIN

Even though their risk and exposure were at an all-time maximum, Eddie desired to grow the business even more, which was not in their best interest. He began to push for more inventory with higher odometer rollbacks for a greater profit margin so that D'Angelo could clean more money and Eddie in turn could be paid more. The greater risk and exposure did not slow Eddie down one bit. He misread things going so smoothly as a sign that he was somehow invincible. After all, Eddie was used to avoiding the cost of consequences. But Jessika would have one last attempt to help him get his feet back on the ground.

"Eddie, how many vehicle shipments are coming in this week?" Jessika inquired.

"Just three or four more," Eddie answered.

"Three or four! Eddie, how are we moving so many cars so fast?"

"We're purchasing distressed vehicles in bulk at a dirt-cheap price, then we're rolling back the odometers so we can sell them for more but for a much lower price than our competitors. So, we're the best show in town. Nobody can beat our prices and we're killing our profit margin," Eddie explained.

"And you don't think that no one is going to ask how we became the number one dealership in America in just a few months!?" Jessika exhorted.

"No, I don't Jessika! In football, the running back runs into the end zone when they make a hole! There's a hole in front of me, Jessika, and I'm running through it!"

This, unfortunately, would be the last chance Eddie would get to check his Hazardous Attitude of Invulnerability. What originally should have brought them 100k a month was generating north of 350k. They were way overexposed and had no clue that they were in the bullseye of the FBI. There were drivers dropping off 18-wheelers full of vehicles that hadn't been vetted. They didn't have time to make sure if inventory was coming from their connect, or Santa Claus in the North Pole for that matter, but Eddie did not seem to care. His mantra became, "Get them in and get them out by any means necessary."

THE JIG IS UP

Eddie hopped in the car and headed to D'Angelo's office. The voice Eddie heard over the phone was a voice of concern but Eddie didn't think much of it. But D'Angelo really didn't ask Eddie to meet. It was more of an "in my office now" kind of moment. As he drove to D'Angelo's office, there was a seesaw going up and down in Eddie's head. In his gut, he knew something was terribly wrong. But the overly optimistic side of him, which was most of him, just wouldn't allow him to give it any more real estate in his being than it had already taken up. After all, he was fully convinced that even though bad consequences occur, they won't ever happen to him. But the sensation intensified, and Eddie almost decided to turn around but before He knew it, he was pulling into the parking lot. As he entered the building, he could sense a level of tension in the air. Like something bad was about to happen. He ignored it again as though he had the ability to will things to a positive outcome. He noticed that the secretary who normally sat by the elevator wasn't there, so he decided to head on up. As the elevator doors opened, Eddie's heart sank. There were more federal agents adorned in polyester jackets with the initials "FBI" than he could possibly count. The room even smelled different. There was an almost penal-type aroma that filled the air as if such a thing ever existed. At this moment Eddie was completely filled with dread, frozen in place, and for the first time in his life, he was scared to death.

His morbid frigidity was awakened by an agent who was now standing so close to him, he could feel his breath on his neck. "Eddie Esposito? Agent John Callahan with the Federal Bureau of Investigation. Please place your hands in front of you." The skin of Eddie's wrists would now experience the rude embrace of cold handcuffs. As Eddie was led away to a shiny black SUV parked behind the building, all kinds of thoughts began to race through his mind. Had he been betrayed by karma? Should he have been more careful? Eddie was the poster child for charisma, good fortune, and luck, and he was now facing a very lengthy prison sentence. With Eddie's help, D'Angelo had laundered more than $2.85MM. The jig was now up. But how could this have happened?

WHAT ABOUT THAT CAR?

It turns out that Eddie didn't know everything about D'Angelo, and D'Angelo didn't know everything about Eddie.

You see Eddie had previously partnered with some members of the Polish community who were into things that were, shall we say, "legal adjacent". It was rare for the Polish to link up with the Italians, but Eddie was no regular guy. He could persuade anybody. Eddie hadn't heard from them in a week or two but he really didn't think anything of it because their partnership was more of a one-off. But the reason why Eddie hadn't heard from them is because, during a sting operation, they were arrested.

It turns out that the car on Eddie's street wasn't just a random car after all. Eddie was being surveilled and he didn't even know it. The only reason he wasn't also arrested is because they hadn't been able to gather enough evidence yet on the level of his involvement. Eddie and Jessika had been surveilled for quite some time now. Including their first meeting with D'Angelo. So instead of Eddie avoiding coming to the authorities because he was now working with D'Angelo, he brought the authorities to D'Angelo's operation with him, and he didn't even know it. D'Angelo was sentenced to ten years in federal prison. Eddie was sentenced to seven. He vehemently claimed that as far as Jessika was concerned, he operated alone and that she had no knowledge or involvement whatsoever. She was let off with just probation. Eddie was now serving time in jail because of his attitude. He thought he was invulnerable to consequences, and he behaved commensurately. Things started out amazing with their operation, but that didn't ensure things would end that way. It's been said that the devil is in the details. My grandmother would say that if you let the devil ride, he'll drive. He'll take you further than you intended to go and have you stay longer than you intended to stay, and have you pay more than you can afford to pay. What about the car you're in? Who's driving?

Invulnerability—"It won't happen to me."
Antidote—Say it out loud: "It could happen to me."
Invulnerability is the Hazardous Attitude that causes people to believe that consequences happen to others, but not to them. It doesn't cross their mind that there is absolutely nothing different about them compared to people who have been casualties of their own actions. They don't have a magic force field around them, but they behave as though they do.

If you let the devil ride, he'll drive. He'll take you further than you intended to go and have you stay longer than you intended to stay, and have you pay more than you can afford to pay.

"Jack be nimble. Jack be quick. Jack jump over the candlestick." These are the words of a popular nursery rhyme that came from England in the 18th century. It's likened to the pirate, Black Jack, who's elusive nature always saved him from being captured by authorities. It was believed that if a person could successfully jump over a lit candlestick without the flame going out, it meant that they would have good fortune and success in their future. Wonderful, right?! Not so fast. Examining the Hazardous Attitude of Invulnerability begs the question, "What happens if the flame goes out?" Here's the truth—we all have acted in a way that would suggest we are invulnerable—from the days of our youth making ramps for our dirt bikes that were not structurally sound to being an adult and pushing the limits on tardiness and missing deadlines with our employer. Still don't agree? If you've had unprotected sex even once in your lifetime, you acted with a Hazardous Attitude of Invulnerability. If we are honest, much of the ills of our society concerning rudderless youth stem from the fact that they were born to parents who had no plan in place whatsoever to rear them. Invulnerability is the one Hazardous Attitude that may cause you to pay a dreadful tax immediately. Let's say you were to buy a ticket on an airline and the captain was known to have a "candlestick mentality" all throughout his training. While on a flight under his/her command, they attempt to land the aircraft under conditions that exceed the aircraft's limitations. I think we would all agree that if the said pilot had a history of displaying a Hazardous Attitude of Invulnerability, we would prefer that they never have pilot credentials in the first place!

I have a question for you: Are there thunderstorms forecasted along your route? Have you been told by people in positions of authority or people who are in community with you to cancel the journey you're on because of the danger it involves? I get it. It's a thin line between knowing when to listen to the people who love you and knowing when to ignore them. One of my favorite podcasts is "How I Built

This", and one of the unifying themes that seems to connect the stories of almost all their guests is that their families or their friends once told them that the idea they had wouldn't work. There's only one thing. . . . it did. These are the stories of entrepreneurs who have been wildly successful in the businesses that they created and almost all had to wrestle with the opinions of people in their circle. They didn't act invulnerable. They simply chose to believe in themselves more than their doubters. A Hazardous Attitude of Invulnerability says, "It won't happen to me" when the data and the odds say otherwise. That's the difference. Let's review how the Hazardous Attitude of Invulnerability was at play in Eddie's life:

ATTITUDE ADJUSTMENTS:

1) A bad case of the "can't help its".

"100,000 dollars a month!?" Eddie immediately looked at Jessika with puppy dog eyes as if to say he had fallen hopelessly in love. Not with her or D'Angelo, but with the idea of making more money in a month than he had made in almost a year. To Eddie, there was nothing more romantic than money—not even Jessika. Eddie quaked and

trembled like an addict. He had heard all that he needed to hear.

Eddie absolutely could not bear the thought of losing the opportunity to make such a large amount of money. People with an Attitude of Invulnerability do not need to hear that there is a reward that will justify their behavior. They often take risks when there is no reward at all.

2) Skill and luck make terrible roommates.

These two had the ability to sell a drowning man a glass of water! They began to have the inventory pour in and they were getting rid of it pretty quickly. D'Angelo's crew was washing more money than Eddie and Jessika could have ever dreamed of. It was almost euphoric. It was as if they were dreaming.

The idea of having a roommate usually creates friction when there are shared responsibilities or lack thereof; meaning, there are usually things expected of the people who live in a shared space, whether it's taking out the trash or loading the dishwasher. Skill and luck make terrible roommates because it seems to become less and less clear who did what. If the person who has a Hazardous Attitude of Invulnerability is also very skillful, like, say, a pilot, then when they aren't met with consequences for behavior that is dangerous, they think that it was because they are skillful . . . when they really just got lucky! This is why skill and luck make terrible roommates.

3) Willful ignorance is the worst kind.

Eddie never asked what kind of business dealings D'Angelo was into or where the money they were cleaning came from. He was willfully ignorant. He just saw this as an opportunity of a lifetime to develop a war chest of cash to do the other things in business that he really wanted to do that required more liquid capital.

When you meet with your employer, a judge, or your spouse about your behavior, it won't go well at all if you willfully turn a blind eye. People are just a lot less empathetic to those who are willfully ignorant. People who have a Hazardous Attitude of Invulnerability will one day need grace. The truth is there will be a lot less available because they were willfully blind.

4) It'll be okay.

"Do you think we're in over our heads?" Jessika cautioned.

"Yeah, I do. I think we're over our heads in cash—what are you talking about, babe?" Eddie responded.

"I mean things seem to be going fine but we're taking risks with cleaning dirty money and rolling back odometers like this is a video game and we have three lives, Eddie."

"Forgive me but I'm not seeing your point, Jessika!"

"The point is, Eddie, that we don't have three lives because God only gave us one life and I don't want to spend the rest of it in jail, you moron!"

As a leader, there are few words that are more frustrating for me to hear than, "It'll be okay." How will it be okay? What has been done to ensure it will be ok? This mindset seems to be medicinal for people who think they are invulnerable. The easiest disposition to gravitate to is, "It'll be ok."

5) It'll never be enough.

They were starting to be bolder in their illegal business affairs. They were rolling back the odometers by larger numbers. They were cleaning money in higher and higher amounts to the point that they didn't care about the inescapable fact that the greedier you get, the more people watch you eat. And people were watching. And when I say people, I mean the Federal Bureau of Investigation.

When the Hazardous Attitude of Invulnerability is coupled with an insatiable appetite, look out. The truth is that if Eddie was bringing in $300MM, he would have dreamed at night what it was like to bring in $400MM. It'll never be enough.

6) The absence of consequence is not the presence of approval.

The greater risk and exposure did not slow Eddie down one bit. He misread things going so smoothly as a sign that he was somehow invincible. After all, Eddie was used to avoiding the cost of consequences. But Jessika would have one last attempt to help him get his feet back on the ground.

When a person thinks they are invulnerable, going through the gauntlet of dangerous behavior without realizing a consequence will only ensure that they will try it again. But never forget, the absence of consequence is not the presence of approval.

7) Chance of a lifetime, or a chance to mess your life up?

"In football, the running back runs into the end zone when they make a hole! There's a hole in front of me, Jessika, and I'm running through it!"

A mirage is a desert phenomenon where the reflection of the heat radiating from the sand's surface looks like an oasis of water. A traveler who is stranded can walk for miles in the direction of what they think is an oasis, only to discover that it is only a mirage. If the "hole" is made possible by reckless behavior, it is only a mirage leading to thirst and death.

Chapter 3

I CAN DO IT: MACHO

E veryone loves a clear day with blue skies. It's almost as if stepping out of the house with the sun shining and the birds singing is an automatic indicator it will be a good day. The presence of sunshine with the absence of rain breeds optimism. There is an old aviation term that is not used anymore called CAVU, pronounced (ca-voo). It means "Ceiling And Visibility Unlimited". A CAVU day is sunny, with no clouds above you and none ahead of you. It's as clear as it can possibly be. It's a beautiful day. How wonderful would it be if life was always filled with CAVU days? Days where the visibility is unlimited, and you knew exactly what would happen next because things go as planned.

We would all love to experience "ceiling unlimited" days where our potential to achieve isn't based on the normal hang-ups and unscheduled disasters that life often throws our way. Our days are not normally "CAVU". Life has a way of "life-ing". And it was not a CAVU day on the ground for certified flight instructor, Hailey Mitchell.

"Where is 62 Alpha?" Hailey asked Buddy, the line mechanic, as she looked for an aircraft with the last three characters of the tail number 6-2-A. This was the airplane she and her student were scheduled to fly that day.

"I took it down for maintenance," Buddy responded.

"Great! All the other planes are checked out!" Hailey informed Buddy. And by "great," she meant terrible. Hailey's student was on the way to the airport for a flight lesson, her aircraft had gone down for maintenance, and she didn't have an adequate ground lesson prepared. This is a regular occurrence in the life of a CFI. General aviation airplanes normally require a lot of maintenance. Students tend to have hard landings all the time because they are learning how to fly. Yet, this is still something that certified flight instructors never get used to.

As her student walked onto the ramp, Hailey was reminded of the need for professionalism her dad taught her and donned a reassuring smile. "Where is 62 Alpha? I need to do my pre-flight check," Hailey's student asked.

"Yeah about that. It just went down for maintenance and all the other planes are booked. So today will be a ground lesson day," Hailey explained. Now, ground lesson days aren't bad at all. They are needed in order for each student pilot to grasp and understand the vast amount of knowledge they are required to know. But when a student is looking forward to flying and they are told that they are staying on the ground, their attitude can shift very fast. Then, Hailey suddenly heard someone yell her name in a promising tone.

"Hailey! 35 Delta just came back on the flight line! You guys can take it," Buddy encouraged.

"YES, we'll take it!" Hailey was full of expectation because she saw the countenance of her student change when the news hit about doing a ground lesson instead of going flying. Hailey said to her student, "Go ahead and preflight 36 Delta and I will be out in about fifteen minutes."

As Hailey's student headed to do the pre-flight checks on the airplane, she went into the break room and began to devour the sandwich she packed for lunch unaware that she wasn't alone.

"Eat often?" Bret, one of Hailey's co-workers, teased.

Hailey rolled her eyes and clapped back, "Have students request to drop you as their instructor often?"

Bret was a good aviator as an individual, but not so much personality-wise. If there was a nerve to touch, he felt as though it was his job to dance on it.

"Yeah, whatever, some people can't handle my level of instruction," Brett replied.

To that, Hailey grinned and walked out of the door.

"Is she airworthy?" Hailey asked her student about the airplane.

"Yep, she's good to go!" Hailey's student pulled out the checklist and began to start the airplane. They then taxied the airplane to an area in the airport called the "run-up" area. This is where the final systems checks are done before approaching the runway for takeoff to make sure the airplane is ready to fly. Line by line, Hailey and her student began to accomplish each item on the Before-Takeoff Checklist. Then all of a sudden, the unfortunate happens.

"Oh crap," Hailey's student remarked.

"Yep. Oh crap," Hailey answered.

When they performed the before-takeoff engine check, the revolutions per minute are supposed to be at 1700rpms, but the engine wouldn't go above 800rpms, which is less than half. This unfortunately meant the engine was not developing enough power to fly.

"Back to the maintenance hangar?"

"Yep. Back to maintenance."

In summary, whoever signed off on 36D coming back on the flight line shouldn't have. At this point, Hailey was a bit annoyed because in her mind they should be flying, or at a minimum, they should be using those precious minutes to conduct a ground lesson so her student could at least gain an ideal level of enrichment from this day. She definitely didn't feel as though she should be taxiing around the airport.

As they pulled up to the maintenance hangar, she was greeted by none other than—nope, not Buddy—Bret!

"Break it already, Hailey?" Bret insulted.

"Still no students, Bret?" Hailey countered.

At this point, Hailey was trying not to show her student how annoyed she was by her seemingly inept co-workers and the overall situation. It was a CAVU day in the air. Though it was a cold thirty-nine degrees, it was still beautiful and sunny with unlimited visibility. If only it were a CAVU day on the ground. "Let's head inside and do a ground lesson," Hailey instructed her student.

Now there weren't many places for ground lessons at Hailey's school. There's the conference room, which is sometimes rented out for meetings for aviation clubs that keep their airplanes in the hangar at the airport. Then there is the break room where Bret hangs out because he doesn't have any students that want him as an instructor. Or there is the owner's office that he doesn't mind CFIs using for ground lessons as long as he is not on a sales call for his real job. Hailey scouted out the various possibilities for a ground lesson location with no success. She was overcome with disappointment. By now it was almost time for her student's lesson to be over.

"Hey I am sorry about this, but there's not much time to get anything done. Let's just call it, okay?" Hailey suggested. In response, her student slumped and walked out the door looking defeated and feeling even worse. To add insult to injury, CFIs do not get paid when they are not instructing. So even though Hailey's student learned an invaluable lesson on spotting a potentially catastrophic engine issue, all the time spent with her student that day would not be billable. Flight instructors get paid to instruct, whether it be ground instruction or flight instruction. Some instructors only get paid for flight instruction. Just as the car tires of Hailey's student peeled out of the parking lot, her boss, the owner, emerged from his office.

"I thought you had a student now, Hailey?" The owner questioned.

"I did but 62 Alpha and 36 Delta both went down for maintenance," Hailey explained.

"And you didn't have a ground lesson prepared?"

At this point, Hailey had no desire to do any more explaining. So, she was thankful that her boss had a low attention span and quickly changed the subject.

"Bret, come in here!" The owner barked. "I am tired of us missing revenue because planes are down. It can't continue. I think I have a solution. I got a call yesterday from Best Avionics. 99 Mike has received new radios and is ready to go. We need as many airplanes as possible, so I need someone to fly it back to base tomorrow morning because we have it scheduled for some afternoon flights."

"I can do it!" Hailey assured.

"Great. You're my pilot to ferry 99 Mike back to base tomorrow morning. If we can get it here by 10 a.m., that would be ideal." Then the owner abruptly retreated to his office, likely to take another sales call.

As Hailey began to look at the weather for the next morning, her heart sank. She realized that she may have bitten off more than she could chew. As Hailey scrolled on her iPad with all her aviation apps, Bret decided to offer commentary. "From the look on your face, you're checking the weather for tomorrow."

"It's fine, nothing I can't handle," Hailey challenged.

"Well if I were you, I would check several times before . . ." As Bret was trying to drop some pearls of wisdom.

Hailey interrupted and said, "I am not you, Bret. You barely have any students and besides, my dad is a Captain at Unity Airlines. He taught me how to fly. Where did you get your license again?" At this point Hailey was stooping far below the level of professionalism she normally operated and that her dad insisted upon.

"Hey, whatever, I was just trying to offer some sound advice. It's your funeral," Bret responded.

Hailey rolled her eyes and simply responded, "I've got it. I can do it."

NO ICE PLEASE

Now you may be wondering what specifically was so bad about the weather that day that had Bret, and even Hailey, concerned. I will explain this in layman's terms the best that I can.

When an airplane is designed by the manufacturer, the wings are designed to have a certain shape. Airplane wings are often flat on the bottom and curved on the top. The shape or design is what causes the wings to provide something called lift, which is one of the four forces that act upon an airplane when it flies through the air. For simplicity purposes, we will deal with just one force and not the other three. The manufacturer knows what minimum airspeed is needed in order for the wing to fly, and that data is a big determining factor in the shape of the wing. Anything that becomes affixed to the wing has now become a part of the wing. For example, if I told you that I changed the shape of the wing of an airplane that you were going to be a passenger on right before your flight, would you board the aircraft? Absolutely not! Well, when the temperatures outside go below freezing the "skin" or the metal on the airplane wings also goes below freezing. Once this happens, if the wing makes contact with precipitation, it will immediately become ice and attach or "affix" itself to the wing, therefore changing the shape and design of the wing. Make sense so far? Good. Here's the big part. The more ice modifications the wing experiences, the more airspeed you will need in order for the wing to fly. If you continue to build ice on the surfaces of the skin of the airplane, at some point it will no longer fly or produce lift no matter how fast you are going because it's no longer shaped the way the manufacturer intended. Ice is bad for airplane wings. Now if you're flying a commercial airline such as Delta, United, American, or Southwest, the Boeing and Airbus jets that they fly have anti-icing gear that is turned on before icing conditions are ideal. However, general aviation airplanes used for training do not have anti-icing equipment. This was the big problem that Hailey was about to face. For small airplanes, ice on the wings is very bad. They just aren't designed to fly that way.

UH OH

We've all had them. Moments inside your gut that tell you to turn around, moments that shout something isn't safe, it's too risky, go the other way, stop now, wait a second, or double check. Hailey was about to have one of these moments. It's how she responded to that moment that would determine her outcome. It's been said that the loudest preacher who exists is the conscience. The voice on the inside of you and me that convicts us and tells us that what we are about to do is harmful. This voice is louder than any outside voice we will ever experience. It often takes great effort to quiet the conscience because the closer you get to danger; it just gets louder and louder. The more we tell the conscience to be quiet, the more it shouts and shouts until it's too late. Why was this an issue of conscience? Because Hailey was about to break the rules of the airplane manufacturer, and her dad had taught her better.

> The more we tell the conscience to be quiet, the more it shouts and shouts until it's too late.

As Hailey exited her Uber at 8:08 a.m., she was greeted by the cold brisk northern Illinois air. She looked up at the sky as pilots often do to look for some sort of visual rebuttal to the weather report she had already received. Not finding any evidence based on the sky condition, she decided to go inside Best Avionics. But before she did, a single mist of moisture tickled her nose. She then looked back and saw her Uber car exiting the airport gate and going down the street, so she decided to head inside.

"Wasn't expecting you guys today," Jim the avionics repairman said to Hailey.

"Yeah, the boss wants 99 Mike back ASAP so I am here to fly her home," Hailey explained.

"Really?"

"Yep. Is she good to go?"

"The airplane, yes, but this weather though . . ."

"Yeah, it's just a little precipitation; nothing to worry about. I can do it."

Even though Jim was not a pilot, he could tell that the weather was, shall we say, less than optimal. But pilots have a designation called "pilot in command" which is often denoted by the acronym PIC. What this means is that if you are the PIC, you are in command or in charge. The responsibility to determine or decide whether or not to operate a flight rest squarely on the shoulders of the PIC in general aviation.

"All you need is a signature, right?" Hailey asked.

"Yep, the price for the repair has already been paid," Jim responded.

Hailey walked out the back door of the shop to the ramp where 99 Mike was parked. She noticed that the airplane had some moisture on the surface, but none was frozen. However, this wasn't a sign that it was safe to fly because the air is colder up at altitude than it is on the ground. The temperature decreases two degrees every 1,000 feet you climb. So, if it's thirty-four degrees on the ground, it's thirty degrees just 2,000 feet in the air, and Hailey would be flying much higher than that. This airport had a control tower so she would have to get clearance to taxi and take off. But first, she obtained her instrument clearance because this would be a flight under instrument flight rules, which meant that Hailey would be in the clouds some or all of her route. She would be flying the airplane solely by the instruments with no reference to the horizon. Hailey then listened to the automated weather recording in her headset. There was no mention of icing, but the present conditions were still optimal for it. Hailey decided it was time to call ground control to get her taxi clearance.

"Ground control, 99 Mike is at Best Avionics with the current weather, ready to taxi," Hailey reported to ground control.

"Uh . . . okay 99 Mike taxi to runway 36 via taxiway Bravo. Stay with me on this frequency," the ground controller instructed hesitantly.

Remember, Hailey is the PIC, not the ground controller. Hailey then repeated the instructions back to the controller but the hesitation in his voice was yet another attempt at Hailey's shouting conscience telling her to turn back. But Hailey's confidence in her piloting skills would override the inner voice telling her it was too dangerous to fly. After all, she can do it, right? Or so she thought. As Hailey approached the hold short line of runway 36, she noticed that the ceiling, the lowest level of cloud cover, had gotten even lower than before when she got out of her Uber. Yet another attempt by her inner voice to get her to turn back. This final attempt would unfortunately fail.

"Tower, 99 Mike is at runway 36 ready for takeoff," Hailey announced.

"99 Mike, Tower, runway 36 clear for takeoff."

As Hailey turned onto the runway, she noticed the outside temperature gauge was now displaying thirty-three degrees but she told herself that wouldn't guarantee that ice would form. Hailey thought to herself, "If I get into trouble, I'll land at a closer airport and wait it out," assuming that she was somehow guaranteed that chance. Hailey lined up with the runway, put the power all the way forward, and began her takeoff roll. With a mighty Cessna 172 roar she rotated and began to fly. It was a beautiful customary takeoff which did not help the situation. Sometimes when even the smallest detail of a larger situation goes as planned, we can take that as evidence all is well. Within seconds Hailey was completely in the clouds flying the airplane solely by the reference of the instruments on the panel in front of her. She's been trained well so she resisted the temptation to look out of the window and get distracted. There's nothing to see because she is in the clouds.

Instrument pilots such as Hailey fly by something called waypoints. Think of it as connecting the dots until you get to the final dot, being the final course for the runway at the airport you're landing at. As Hailey reached her first waypoint, she also reached her assigned altitude. She cruised along headed to her home base and everything about the flight so far was good. She looked at her engine gauges and they were good. She looked at her pressure levels and they were good. She looked at her heading and altitude and both were perfect. Becoming preoccupied with all of the normal aspects of flying, Hailey was interrupted by the outside air temperature gauge, which was now reading twenty-eight degrees, far below thirty-two degrees. Looking at the wing struts and the wings, everything looked fine. It was at that moment she reassured herself that, "I've got this." She thought Bret definitely couldn't do it and her boss would be thankful she flew 99 Mike back to her home base. Hailey was putting her aviation skills on full display, or so she intended.

All of a sudden, the controls became a little sluggish. As a trained instrument pilot, she was gentle with the controls to not cause the airplane to oscillate. As her tail beacon bounced off the clouds, she noticed that the reflection on the airplane was shinier than it should have been. Hailey's heart sank; she was picking up ice on her wings. The next thing that happened was, she heard a sound that no pilot in this situation wants to hear. The stall warning horn began to chirp. This is the warning that a stall of the wing is imminent. Why would the wing stall though? Because by flying the airplane through icing conditions, the ice was changing the manufacturer's design by affixing itself to the wings. Ice on the wing of an airplane destroys lift, which is the force that keeps you from going down. Hailey added power and took the engine from 2200rpms to 2400rpms and for a moment, the stall warning horn went off. Hailey then breathed a sigh of relief, but only for a moment. She started to look for a closer airport to land at but the closest one was ten miles away. Ice had also begun to form around her pitot tube which was this airplane's only way of telling her how fast she was going. Then the regrettable happened. Yep, the stall warning horn came back. This was because the wings were losing their ability to generate lift because they were covered in clear ice. Hailey then put the power all the way forward—she gave it everything she had. Think of putting the power forward as stepping all the way down on the gas pedal in your car.

Unfortunately, giving the airplane more power didn't do it and it began to flutter. At this point, Hailey did what any pilot would do. She began to look for a field or any soft place to land but she couldn't see a thing because she was completely engulfed in murky clouds. Hailey tried her best to control the airplane under these impossible conditions, but to no avail. As Hailey tried to correct the inevitable, she caused the airplane to stall, then the left wing dipped, and it nosed over into a spin. As Hailey spiraled to the ground there was a glimpse of light that burst through the flight deck at about 600 feet above the ground. You may be thinking to yourself, if only she had seen a breakthrough in the clouds before 600 feet. That thought is problematic for one important reason. You should be thinking, if only she had chosen not to fly. As 99 Mike plummeted the final 600 feet, the right wing clipped a light pole and separated it from the fuselage. The airplane came to rest at the foot of the wooden pole, and Hailey did not survive the crash.

THE AFTERMATH

As always with an aircraft accident, there was a full investigation. But the only person who truly knew all of the details was now deceased and the answers would have to wait, leaving many people who knew and loved Hailey wondering how this could have happened. Even Bret was showing signs of guilt and remorse for not saying more or insisting she shouldn't fly. But after all, Hailey was PIC.

Hailey's boss, however, filed an insurance claim for the aircraft 99 Mike and put out a hiring ad for a certified flight instructor the same week. Yep, what a piece of work he was. Out of sight, out of mind. On the day of Hailey's funeral, there was a sea of Unity Airlines pilots in uniform seated in the church to the left of the pulpit in support of their co-worker, Hailey's dad. Though they were professional commercial pilots flying for a legacy airline, they were no different from Hailey. Many of them knew what it was like to have an over-inflated sense of self-ability at one point in time. The only difference is they were fortunate enough to live to tell their story. The eulogist stood up and walked to the pulpit to honor Hailey and make his best attempt at encouraging her family. He did so beautifully, and her dad even laughed as he told stories of Hailey growing up and how she had such an admiration for flying. But he also challenged those left behind. The eulogist was not only a pastor, but he was also a pilot himself. It may seem harsh to some, but since there were so many pilots present at Hailey's funeral, he could not let this chance to challenge them go unclaimed. If he did lose this opportunity, it could mean losing another pilot. He reminded them that most pilots who die in bad weather conditions are buried on clear and sunny days. On the day of Hailey's funeral, it was CAVU in the air but not on the ground.

Macho—"I can do it."

Antidote—Say it out loud: "Taking unnecessary risks is foolish."

Macho is an attitude that is found in people who constantly feel the need to prove themselves. They often think they are better or more skilled than everyone else and they desire to live in the hall of fame of "one-ups". Their mantra is "hold my beer." They often see the risk they are taking as worth it, while everyone around them sees the risk as foolish. It is the attitude of a person with an over-inflated sense of self-ability.

ATTITUDE ADJUSTMENTS

1) **Keep calm and stay right side up.**

   At this point Hailey is trying not to show her student how annoyed she is by her seemingly inept co-workers and the overall situation. It was a CAVU day in the air. Though it was a cold thirty-nine degrees, it was still beautiful and sunny with unlimited visibility. If only it were a CAVU day on the ground."

Whenever a Hazardous Attitude of Macho surfaces in a way that is potentially dangerous, it's usually after a series of unfortunate uncontrollable events. A person with an over-inflated sense of self-ability or macho attitude will often try to overcompensate for that which they can control, causing them to respond in dangerous ways. Pilots are often told to keep the airplane right side up, meaning fly the airplane first. Don't get distracted and get upside down. Don't allow the things you cannot control to cause you to overreact to the things you can control.

2) Give yourself the gift of saying, "I changed my mind."

"I am tired of us missing revenue because planes are down. It can't continue. I think I have a solution. I got a call yesterday from Best Avionics. 99 Mike has received new radios and is ready to go. We need as many airplanes as possible, so I need someone to fly 99 Mike back to base tomorrow morning because we have it scheduled for some afternoon flights," the owner informed.

"I can do it!" Hailey assured.

"I can do it" is the mantra of the macho. Haley did not have all the weather information when she said these famous words. You know what happens next. Give yourself the gift of saying, "I changed my mind." When you "write a check that you can't cash", just own up. Re-adjust and don't double down. It could mean that you avert experiencing a life-altering consequence.

3) Let it go.

As Hailey scrolled on her iPad with all her aviation apps, Bret decided to offer commentary. "From the look on your face, you're checking the weather for tomorrow."

"It's fine, nothing I can't handle," Hailey challenged.

"Well if I were you, I would check several times before . . ." As Bret was trying to drop some pearls of wisdom, Hailey interrupted and said, "I am not you, Bret. You barely have any students and besides, my dad is a Captain at Unity Airlines. He taught me how to fly. Where did you get your license again?" At this point Hailey was stooping far below the level of professionalism she normally operated and that her dad insisted upon.

"Hey, whatever, I was just trying to offer some sound advice. It's your funeral," Bret responded.

Hailey rolled her eyes and simply responded, "I've got it. I can do it."

Holding on to offense and unforgiveness against someone is like drinking poison and hoping that they die. It's insanity. Let it go. If you ever want to see a Hazardous Attitude of Macho metastasize, offend the macho person, doubt their ability. Remember that taking unnecessary risks is foolish.

Chapter 4

DO SOMETHING: IMPULSIVITY

HURRY UP!

The game of charades has been around for decades. It's a game where people do everything they can to guess what the player in front of them is illustrating. The sound that you hear is normally very loud because people say and do the first thing that comes to mind in fear of missing out on the chance to guess the correct answer. To be impulsive goes hand-in-hand with the game of charades. It's one of the things about the game that makes it so entertaining. The game moves so fast that there isn't much time to think about what you're shouting out or gesturing, so the people playing charades often look and sound very silly. And it's okay! Because it's just a game. When you're playing charades, it's perfectly okay to look and sound ridiculous, saying or doing the first thing that comes to mind as you work on either illustrating or guessing the correct answer.

Speaking out of turn, saying or doing something without thinking it through, and being impulsive are inherently a part of the game of charades. But it's a terrible way to run a business. And this was the norm for CEO Tharen Dylan. Whatever came to mind, he did. Whatever he felt, he said. It didn't matter how much risk it would expose his company to or how inappropriate it was. Tharen lived a life without a filter whether in word or in deed. And in the event of a stressful moment, his usual response was to do the first thing that came to mind. The decisions we make in life should be filtered through taking time to think about our actions. When a person faces a problem, and they do the first thing that comes to mind without thinking first, that's the Hazardous Attitude of Impulsivity. Tharen was as impulsive as a person could be. And each time nothing catastrophic happened to him as a result of his impulsivity, it only made him more impulsive.

Now you may ask, *how does a CEO work their way up the rigorous corporate ladder in the business world to become a CEO if they are wildly impulsive*? Well, Tharen is the CEO of the companies he created. So why would people choose to follow him? I need to tell you up front that Tharen may be impulsive, but he's not an idiot—there's a difference. Tharen actually gained prominence for his impulsive nature. His impulsivity led to some business dealings that paid off generously. When other people hesitated at an opportunity that presented itself, Tharen's impulsive nature caused him to act fast, and he lucked out bigtime. It's sorta like a football coach who always decides to go for it on 4th down. If it mostly works, then he's a hero. If it doesn't, then he's likely fired. Tharen's gut instincts usually lead him to throw "Hail Marys" toward the end zone rather than slow methodical gains down the field of business. The Hazardous Attitude of Impulsivity is the response that leads people to do something—anything—quickly without thinking it through. If their rash decision works, it only increases their probability of being impulsive in the future with even greater risks. If it doesn't work, especially after a long-established history of impulsivity, the cost is usually very high. Lessons that are learned the latest are usually learned hardest.

Tharen was a technology genius. That was his industry of choice where he made his mark. If only the investors knew how often his impulsive nature had caused the companies he ran to stare death in the face. Tharen was not unlike many other budding entrepreneurs turned CEOs who have fallen to the Hazardous Attitude of Impulsivity. He just had not fallen as of yet.

Lessons that are learned the latest are usually learned hardest.

ON THE ROAD AGAIN

It was 8:08 a.m. and Tharen's driver was waiting patiently outside his residence to drive him to the airport. Tharen was normally on time unless there was something else more interesting that captured his attention. Just when Jon, Tharen's driver, was about to ring the doorbell a second time, out came Tharen dressed in his customary white t-shirt, black blazer, blue jeans, and a pair of fresh black sneakers with white trim. To Jon's surprise, Tharen did not seem to be his normal happy-go-lucky self. So, as they pulled off and headed to the airport, Jon decided to inquire.

"How's it going today, Mr. Dylan?" Jon asked.

"It could be better. When you're dealing with people, progress is delayed unnecessarily at times," Tharen commented.

"New project you're working on?" Jon asked.

"Yeah we need to branch out to a few other sectors but it's taking too long to get in position," Tharen retorted.

"Position how?"

"Meaning every time there's a window of opportunity that comes open, there's too much explaining that has to be done to key personnel, and by the time the explaining process is over, the opportunity is less interesting to me."

"I see."

Jon responded with the words "I see", but he really didn't "see". He knew that Tharen's conglomerate of companies were worth millions of dollars. What could be so urgent that he needed his team to get in position without any explanation or thought? Now Jon was more than Tharen's driver;

Jon was also Tharen's quasi-counselor. Tharen trusted Jon though he rarely listened to anyone. Jon knew enough about his boss to know that it was probably his impulsive nature that was causing Tharen's perceived delays.

Team members, whether they be peers or subordinates, must have confidence in the person they are following, and impulsive people erode confidence. And when you have companies as large as Tharen's, even though you're the CEO, you can't exactly move with complete autonomy. There are shareholders and voting board seats to consider. There is a marketing and communications department to filter messaging through. There is a legal department that exists to keep key personnel out of jail or from being sued. By now you get the point. Large infrastructure companies do not move swiftly on a whim and Jon understood that even if CEO Tharen Dylan did not. Tharen's next request would try Jon's patience a tad bit.

"Hey, can you swing by Bella's?" Tharen asked Jon. Bella's was an amazing donut shop that usually had a line. It's so good that they usually sell out every morning by 10 a.m. There's only one problem. Tharen was on his way to the airport.

"Bella's?" Jon clarified.

"Yeah, the strawberry donut is calling my name."

"Mr. Dylan, we are cutting it close to your flight, don't you think?" Jon reasoned.

"Yeah, but we'll be fine, and besides, I really want a strawberry donut."

Not wanting to waste any more time than they already had, Jon pointed the car in the direction of Bella's Donuts. What do you think they saw when they arrived? You guessed it, a line! As they pulled up, Jon was feverishly trying to think of the perfect combination of words to reason with Tharen. Just when he was about to speak, Tharen had already opened the door and was immediately recognized by one of his fans who happened to be in the front of the line.

"Hey that's Tharen Dylan!" someone shouted from the front of the line.

"Hey, buddy," Tharen responded with a rockstar-like tone.

"Can I get a picture?"

"Sure thing."

As Tharen obliged his request, he offered to allow him to go first in line. Jon then breathed a sigh of relief, while also being annoyed that yet another one of Tharen's impulsive gambles worked in his favor. Besides, how did Tharen know that one of his fans would be in the front of the line and let him butt in anyway? That question would have to wait. Jon was becoming less enthused because he knew they needed to get back on their way to the airport ASAP.

"Mr. Dylan, we really need to be on our way sir, if you're going to make your flight." Jon counseled.

Whenever he would correct Tharen, he would be sure to call him "sir." Tharen grabbed his strawberry donut and hopped back into the car. "Okay my friend, off we go!" Tharen said, as though it were his idea to get going to the airport. Jon was careful to make sure his face was pointed toward the steering wheel before he rolled his eyes.

On their way to the airport, Jon all but broke some laws to get him there on time. Jon had to get his daughter from swim practice after dropping Tharen off at the airport. That would be hard to do if he also had to drive him all the way home because he missed his flight. As they pulled up to the departing flight's drop-off area, Jon really didn't know whether to stay or leave at that point. As he turned around to talk to Tharen, all he saw was the back of his jacket, "Bye now, Jon!" Tharen grabbed his bag and hopped out of the car as quickly as he had gotten in. There was, however, a half-eaten strawberry donut left on his seat. At the sight of the donut, Jon scoffed and scooped it into the trash. As Tharen approached his gate, he noticed that the first-class passengers had already boarded.

"Excuse me, Miss, has boarding already begun?" Tharen asked.

"Yes, sir, boarding began ten minutes ago. Where are you seated?" The desk agent replied.

"I'm first class but now there are people in front of me," Tharen responded not considering that more than twenty minutes was eaten up by the pointless pursuit of his half-eaten donut. Tharen boarded the flight and found his seat. Though he was now settled, things at the office were far from serene.

THE WATER COOLER

"Hey man, did you get that email late last night from Tharen?" Doug asked Jason.

"Which one? As a matter of fact, all of the emails I seem to get from him are late at night. And he wants a response before I get to work in the morning. Like I don't sleep," Jason commented.

Well according to Tharen, we shouldn't be sleeping, not unless we want to be losers and allow other companies to beat us," Doug mentioned.

"I hear you," Jason affirmed.

"He wants to branch out to other sectors and acquire some more companies and not much research has been done."

"It's really hard to follow someone who is so impulsive."

"Like the time he decided that the entire office should work on the outside lawn for a day with no coordination with the facilities department or checking the forecast?"

"Exactly!" Jason acknowledged.

"My intern was completely soaked from head to toe. You should have seen her face when she walked past the mirror in the lobby," Doug joked.

"Or how about the time he decided on a whim to do an off-site one week prior?" Jason recalled.

Now you may be thinking that it's impossible to be super impulsive and also rise to success. Not so. You have to remember that some people are just lucky enough to not have any life-ending blow-ups . . . well, yet. Tharen's leadership style was wholly Tharen. Meaning, if it made sense to him, then it made real sense. If it felt right to him, then it must have been right. Impulsivity doesn't have time to consider other people, let alone the repercussions of the actions taken. While the world may know Tharen as a genius CEO who just happens to seem like a gambling risk-taker, the people close to him have experienced him very differently. To them, his genius has worn off and they are becoming fatigued with the constant vacillations that are a part of operating within his orbit. A person with an impulsive nature will always affect the people around them, but they rarely have time to notice it. Jason and Doug both play an integral role in Tharen's conglomerate of companies, but neither had much trust in his character despite their high level of confidence in his intelligence. Again, Tharen is not limited at all mentally, however, he is very limited behaviorally and that's exactly what a Hazardous Attitude is. It's an attitude that causes a person to behave or respond to a situation in a way that is hazardous.

A person with an impulsive nature will always affect the people around them, but they rarely have time to notice it.

Meanwhile, Tharen was at the airport and had boarded his flight. The door was closed, and they had already pushed back from the gate. There was only one problem: absolutely nothing was happening, or so it seemed. Air Traffic Control had notified the crew of Tharen's flight that there was lightning and thunderstorms in the vicinity of the airport and all ground and flight operations had to cease. The tension in the aircraft was palpable as people considered how long this delay might be or whether this flight would even take off in the first place. And then came the dreaded overhead announcement, "Folks this is the captain speaking to you from the flight deck," *insert excessively long exhale*, "I wish I had better news for you but the tower has notified us that we are unfortunately ground stopped. We don't know for how long, and we cannot return to the gate at this time. So please be patient and stay in your seat with your seatbelts securely fastened because as soon as we are permitted to move, we will."

The captain might as well have told Tharen that the crew would be coming through the cabin shortly to give prostate exams. He was furious as though someone should have planned for this. He began to feverishly look out of the window, back at the gate, up front toward the flight deck, and then out of the window again. As if shaking his head violently was going to cause the airplane to begin to move. And that's the moment when Tharen started "Tharening."

"Excuse me, ma'am." Tharen addressed the flight attendant. "How long will it be before we takeoff?"

Looking puzzled because the captain just finished speaking to the passengers, the flight attendant thought she should be poised and polite and repeat the announcement again. "Sir there has been a ground stop due to lightning and thunderstorms in the vicinity of the airport and we don't know how long we are delayed at this time."

"But do we have a time is what I am asking? A time that we will be wheels up?"

Now at this point, the flight attendant was thinking to herself, *If this guy speaks English, surely he just understood what I said.* Nevertheless, the kind flight attendant decided to make attempt number two. "Sir we don't have a time but as soon as we do we will let you know." She then put her feet one in front of the other, and Tharen rolled his eyes. He decided to call the office to vent about his horrible trip, but he wasn't prepared to hear what he would hear next.

"Hello! Hello Jason?" Tharen greeted.

"Hi Tharen, how are you?" Jason answered.

"Not very good," Tharen replied. "I am stuck on the ramp at the airport due to weather and we can't go back to the gate and we can't take off. It's like I am being held hostage or something."

"Oh wow, I am sorry to hear that. Now is probably not the time but we just got a call from Cynos, the company we are negotiating with for an acquisition. They said they have to have an answer by 4 p.m. today."

"4 p.m. today!?" Tharen challenged.

"Yes. You know how I feel about knee-jerk deals," Jason cautioned.

"Yeah well, we are not the ones doing the knee jerking. We're the ones getting jerked. And this is something we already talked about, so I say we go all in."

At this point, several things are happening at once. Jason is rolling his eyes and sighing in an overly dramatic fashion while other people in the office try to guess what the conversation is about. It's obvious from his plum-like face that he is talking to Tharen, without question. Tharen is on his flight that isn't flying and speaking in a volume that is inappropriate for close quarters in a public place. The flight attendants are pulling straws to see who will get the honor to go and tell him to be quiet. The passengers are looking on as if to say, "If the flight attendants don't tell him to be quiet, we will." Jason has had time to breathe and is now ready to respond.

"Tharen, when you say 'all in,' I am pretty sure I know what you mean, but please clarify that for me."

"When I say all in, I mean all in! Make them an offer they can't refuse! Show them we are in charge! I'm tired of all these delays!" Tharen shouted.

"What delays?" Jason challenged.

"Every time we get ready to take on a new venture there is just too much delay and explanation happening where there should be progress. It's pathetic!"

At the sound of Tharen escalating his voice even more, the flight attendant rose to her feet and gracefully made her way to 3C. That would be Tharen's seat. "Sir, I am going to have to ask you to discontinue your call."

"Okay, well when you ask me, I will," Tharen snapped at the flight attendant.

Now at this point the other passengers aren't nearly as consumed by the delay. They are enjoying their metaphorical "popcorn" and sitting on the edge of their seats. But we'll have to come back to that because Jason was about to respond.

"Tharen, it's not pathetic to think before we act," Jason cautioned.

"What is there to think about!" Tharen challenged Jason. "We have the money! It's a good company! And they have set a deadline so let's go all in! What's so hard to understand about that?"

Since Tharen has clearly refused to obey instructions, one of the male flight attendants twice Tharen's size decided to engage. "Sir, get off the phone now." The other passengers that were previously on the edge of their seats were now sitting on air.

"Fine, whatever," Tharen said to the male flight attendant twice his size. "I've got to go," Tharen explained to Jason.

As the flight attendant walked away, Tharen sized him up and thought to himself whether he had done enough CrossFit to take him. Then his phone buzzed. It was a text message from Jason which read, "Have you seen their balance sheet since the last time we reviewed it a month ago?" Now, in Tharen's eyes, the text message Jason sent might as well said, "Delay delay delay delay . . ." Tharen responded, "No I have not Jason! Have you! We don't need to see the balance sheet if we know they are good, and they're good!" This was exactly the kind of response that Jason expected from Tharen but it prepared him nonetheless. "Well, what about their stocks? Do we know if they've dumped any this morning, and maybe that's the reason for the abrupt deadline?" Jason texted in response to Tharen. At this point Tharen is completely annoyed by Jason and Jason is equally annoyed by Tharen. This conversation was going bad and at a very fast pace. "Nobody would be that crazy to dump a bunch of stock and then bump up a deadline! Who would fall for that anyway! I'm done with this!" Tharen retorted.

Jason breathed a sigh of relief when he read the words, "I'm done with this" in Tharen's text. He didn't want to continue this text brawl any more than a person would want a hole in their head. But Tharen wasn't exactly done because he got another impulse. The first impulse was to risk missing his flight to get a strawberry donut from Bella's, that he left on his driver's rear car seat. The second impulse was to go "all in" on a deal that still needed to be fully vetted. Impulse number three would be a doozy.

"Excuse me, ma'am, I really need to make a phone call," Tharen said to the female flight attendant who was not twice his size.

"Sir, your phone privileges have already been restricted due to your volume." The flight attendant said to Tharen.

"Yes I understand, but we are delayed just sitting here and I have to make a very important phone call," Tharen pleaded with the flight attendant.

"I'm sorry, sir. Hopefully, we will get on our way soon, but you cannot use your cell phone."

At the sound of her ruling, Tharen was disappointed. But not too disappointed because he could still text. Tharen was about to do something that was impulsively negligent. He was about to circumvent his team to go directly to the owner of Cynos, Todd David, to cut a deal. All on impulse. All over text message. While sitting on the ramp on a plane that had been delayed by weather. This was a terrible impulse and a Hazardous Attitude. The heat of the moment was causing Tharen to make a bad choice. He was fed up with Jason causing what he perceived was yet another delay. He was fed up with God over the weather pattern that persisted in delaying them. He was fed up with the flight crew that had restricted his phone privileges. If there is one thing that you and I must learn about impulsive people, it's that stress doesn't cause them to thrive; it causes them to dive. And by that, I mean dive deeper into trouble.

Tharen thought for a moment, which, as usual, wasn't long enough. He typed Todd a text message, "Hey buddy got your deadline. I can make that happen." And then he hit "send". What a terrible impulsive nature. Is Tharen accountable to anyone? Technically, yes. Did he build his companies by himself? No. But his message to Todd is, "I can make it happen." All on impulse. All on the spur of the moment. When Todd received Tharen's text, he began to salivate. Why? Because he knows Tharen to be highly impulsive. And he also understands that he's got Tharen right where he wants him, acting on impulse and not on a well-thought-out plan.

"I didn't think I would be hearing from you directly, Tharen. How do we make this official?" Todd responded.

"I am prepared to make you an offer that will be very convincing so we can close this out," Tharen texted Todd.

"That's what I like to hear. Shoot!" Todd responded back.

Todd understands exactly what's happening, though Tharen does not. Tharen should not be brokering an acquisition deal by himself, let alone over text messaging, but alas, he was. At this moment, Tharen did something that Todd did not expect him to do. He asked a follow-up question "Hey man, can I ask why the sudden move up on the deadline?" Tharen inquired. Now this is one of those questions that Todd knew ahead of time he would have to answer, so he was prepared with his response. He just didn't anticipate the question coming from "Mr. Impulsive" himself. Todd knows that as long as he strokes Tharen's ego, he's home-free. Todd then responds, "Tharen, I respect you and we have a long-standing business relationship. I have other aggressive offers on the table, but I wanted to give you the chance to say yes or no because you are the genius that this company needs to go to the next level. Despite the amount of money with other deals, you're the best CEO." If there is one thing impulsive people do not need around them, it's people rationalizing their impulsivity. Obviously, Todd hasn't texted anything at all Tharen would disagree with. Tharen felt that he was the best option too. This exchange of flattery was all Todd needed to close the deal.

"We'll go all in at a purchase price of $1 billion for Cynos. How does that sound?" Tharen offered over text.

Now on the other end of the phone, Todd David, CEO of Cynos, has a fluttering heart with a sheepish grin. He knows that Tharen's company has the money, but he also knows that Tharen is being highly impulsive and flying solo at this point. "We can make that work. It's a solid offer. All we need to get things started is a simple letter of intent with the purchase price. Once I have that I will submit it to our partners and we'll consider Cynos off the market."

Though it was not yet official, all the signs were there that Tharen had just bought a company for $1 billion that he didn't really plan to buy that day when he woke up. Talk about an impulse buy. As Tharen sat in his seat looking around at all of the "less fortunate people" who didn't just buy a billion-dollar company via text message, he crossed his legs, folded his arms, and sat back in his seat, breathing a sigh of relief. That was until he heard the next overhead announcement from the flight deck.

"Folks this is your captain speaking; we have been cleared for takeoff. Make sure your seatbelts are securely fastened."

After that announcement, the airplane started to move under its own power down the taxiway. People began to cheer and clap loudly, the flight attendants began to smile again, and everyone was so happy! Well almost everyone. Everyone except for Tharen. It was now 3:53 p.m. and the airplane was moving closer and closer to the assigned runway for takeoff. If Tharen did not receive and return the signed letter of intent from Todd before the plane took off, the deal was off and Todd could go with another offer.

"Excuse me. Miss. Is there any way we can delay the takeoff?" Tharen pleaded to the first-class flight attendant.

"Excuse me, sir, are you kidding? We are taxiing to the runway right now and the only thing that could stop us is an emergency," The flight attendant advised Tharen.

Now at this point, it's 3:55 p.m. and Tharen is literally considering the return on investment of paying a hefty fine for faking a medical emergency to delay the takeoff. His mind was going back and forth like a "see-saw" thinking of what kind of emergency he could cause that would stop the flight but not land him in jail. At 3:57 p.m., they are number three in line for takeoff, meaning there are only two planes ahead of them, and Tharen's phone beeps. "Yes!!!!" Tharen screamed on the plane as the flight attendant looked super confused thinking that he didn't want to fly. Tharen received the letter of intent from Todd. This was everything he wanted. With this document, Tharen would secure the deal. There was only one problem—Todd's attorney was no novice. He included two spaces for board members on the final page for signatures. It's now 3:58 p.m. and Tharen's flight is number one for takeoff.

Tharen would now do his most impulsive act of all. He used his smartphone to screenshot the signature page.

Just as the clock struck 3:59 p.m., the pilot turned onto the runway and Tharen hit the edit button on the photo, drew his signature, and forged the signatures of the other board members. As the airplane bounced down the runway, he attached it to a text message to Todd and hit send just as the wheels left the ground. By the time Todd saw the email with Tharen's response, thirty minutes had passed. He wasn't exactly waiting with bated breath. Why is that? It's because there were never any other buyers in the first place. Tharen had been finessed. He was visibly perspiring as his flight began to climb. His pulse was raging and his breathing was labored, but he was full of a euphoric-like exhilaration because his impulsivity had paid off yet another time, or so he thought.

Todd was in no hurry at all to preserve Tharen's reputation or business relationships with his board. He was after Tharen's money and nothing else. There was never any type of non-disclosure agreement attached to the letter of intent. He immediately began to brag to his team that he had just inked the deal of a lifetime. As always, word traveled fast, so fast that a source close to Cynos shared the news with FNN (Financial News Network). The news of the Cynos acquisition was meteoric in the headlines and on social media. It was dead that night as far as breaking news goes, so this shot right to the top. Unbeknownst to Tharen, a media fire was burning under him as he flew to his destination. As his flight landed and taxied to the gate, he could sense that something was not right but he couldn't put his finger on what. It's amazing how taking time to pause and think will give great clarity in even the murkiest of situations. Tharen was first on the jet bridge into the terminal. What he saw on the TV screen gave witness to what he was feeling in his gut. There on the terminal TV read a news headline from FNN, "Breaking News: Cynos acquired by CEO Tharen Dylan in $1 Billion Acquisition Deal." Tharen's heart sank. He knew he had messed up. How would he explain this to his board? How would he explain this to his team? How would he explain this to a child, for that matter? Impulsive people often act immediately and are met with immediate regret. What Tharen did next is what he should have done first; he paused, sat down in a chair in the terminal as he stared at the screen, and began to think about what he would do. If only he had done this two hours ago! He wouldn't have time to think long because his phone began to ring profusely. With every answered ring there was another beep on the line.

VP after VP. Board member after board member called Tharen for the next twenty-seven minutes. Tharen did his best to answer everyone but the barrage of incoming calls overwhelmed him. He decided to turn his phone off and walk over to the bar.

> Impulsive people often become victims of their own luck.

Tharen's impulsivity would not allow him to go unscathed this time. This was a bad deal that was also completely avoidable. It turns out that Todd was trying to dump a company with cooked books and an overinflated valuation, and Tharen was his sucker of choice. Fortunately, the legal team that works for Tharen's conglomerate of companies was able to stop the deal based on Tharen's forgery of board member signatures. The good news is that they avoided a major pitfall from a bad deal. The bad news is that the board voted Tharen out as CEO, and he subsequently lost his board seat. He was still a very rich man, but he

128 · RICKY BROWN

was ousted by the companies he founded for being wildly impulsive which led him to do something illegal. This story is not at all unheard of. Impulsive people often become victims of their own luck. Little do they know that the more they jump over the proverbial candlestick without blowing it out, the closer they get to being burned.

———

Impulsivity—"Do it quickly!"
Antidote—Say it out loud: "Not so fast, think first."

Impulsivity is the attitude of people who feel the need to do something—anything—immediately. They don't think first before acting and generally do the first thing that comes to mind without weighing the consequences or taking the time to select the best choice. This is especially true in stressful, high-stakes circumstances. Pilots can fall prey to this when they have an engine out. Instead of verifying the engine that needs to be secured and fully shut down, they inadvertently shut down the good engine. (Yes, this has happened.) Impulsivity prefers to act first over thinking first. Let's review some ways that Tharen showed signs of impulsivity so that we can learn from his mistakes without paying for the lesson ourselves.

ATTITUDE ADJUSTMENTS

1) See people as partners and not speed bumps.

"How's it going today, Mr. Dylan?" Jon asked.

"It could be better. When you're dealing with people, progress is delayed unnecessarily at times," Tharen commented.

"New project you're working on?" Jon inquired.

"Yeah, we need to branch out to a few other sectors but it's taking too long to get in position," Tharen retorted.

"Position how?"

"Meaning every time there's a window of opportunity that comes open, there's too much explaining that has to be done to key personnel, and by the time the explaining process is over, the opportunity is less interesting to me."

Individuals who have the Hazardous Attitude of Impulsivity will tend to see people as speed bumps and not partners. Once they have experienced the spark of an idea, anyone who is not catapulting them toward their newfound genius is viewed as an enemy. This is especially harmful because the people around them are usually their only saving grace to get them to pause, think, and behave rationally. How might you begin to see the people around you differently?

2) It's the little foxes that spoil the vine.

"Hey, can you swing by Bella's?" Tharen asked Jon. Bella's was an amazing donut shop that usually had a line. It's so good that they usually sell out every morning by 10 a.m. There's only one problem. Tharen was on his way to the airport.

"Bella's?" Jon clarified.

"Yeah, the strawberry donut is calling my name."

"Mr. Dylan, we are cutting it close for your flight, don't you think?" Jon reasoned.

"Yeah, but we'll be fine, and besides, I really want a strawberry donut."

Impulsive people are usually impulsive on every level. Meaning, it's not just about the big illegitimate acquisitions over text messaging that you have to worry about. But the "strawberry donut days" in the lives of impulsive people work to reinforce their identity as a person who has the Hazardous Attitude of Impulsivity. Remember, when the situation is a high-stress, high-stakes scenario, it usually means all bets are off. But how can you begin to notice the strawberry donuts in your impulsive habits? By recognizing these small moments that are not nearly as emotionally charged as a merger or acquisition, you can begin to recognize this kind of behavior in yourself during the big moments, as well. Saying no to the strawberry donut on the way to the airport can be more powerful than you might think.

> By recognizing small moments that are not nearly as emotionally charged, you can begin to recognize this kind of behavior in yourself during the big moments, as well.

3) If it's gotta be now, it's gotta be no.

Tharen would now do his most impulsive act of all. He used his smartphone to screenshot the signature page. Just as the clock struck 3:59 p.m., the pilot turned onto the runway, Tharen hit the edit button on the photo, drew his signature, and forged the signatures of the other board members. As the airplane bounced down the runway, he attached it to a text message to Todd and hit send just as the wheels left the ground.

The countdown of the clock did not help Tharen's decision-making at all. In fact, it was the single greatest external factor that led him to make a terrible decision that also happened to be illegal. External factors that create stress and intensify situations are huge red flags that it's time to pause and think about what we are about to do. If you suffer from impulsivity, now might be the time for a new mantra: "If it's gotta be now, it's gotta be no."

Chapter 5

WHAT'S THE USE: RESIGNATION

A THOUSAND CUTS

It's the death of a thousand cuts. That's what it's like to fall prey to the Hazardous Attitude of Resignation for a pastor. Meaning it is usually not one catastrophic thing that causes a pastor to throw in the towel, but it's the constant and continual "nicks" over many decades of ministry. Sure, being a pastor is more of a calling than it is a career, but there is still a desire to have fruit or success. The difference is what makes a pastor feel fruitful or successful versus a business owner or real estate investor for example. It's not the accolades or achievements that laud him or her as being successful, it's when those who are part of the congregation and placed under their charge flourish. That's when a pastor feels most effective.

A pastor is a shepherd. A shepherd is a sheep herder. The sheep are the people of the congregation. If one of the sheep wanders off and is eaten by a wolf, the pastor feels deeply responsible and mournful as they should. (If they don't have a deep sense of loss when a sheep is eaten by a wolf then they are not a pastor and should immediately find something else to do.) My point is that even though the pastor did not lead the sheep to the wolf and feed the sheep to it, there is still an overwhelming weight of responsibility for those who have been placed under their charge as a shepherd. Now I understand being eaten by a wolf is a bit dramatic and most people will never experience that, so let's use examples that are more realistic.

How about when a pastor spends hours developing a sermon series on the biblical principles of marriage and relationships but some under their care enter into harmful relationships, break their marriage vows, and file for divorce? Did the pastor destroy their marriage? No. Do they feel a great sense of responsibility? Of course, they do.

Or how about teaching the biblical principles of financial stewardship only to watch some hearers struggle beyond the normal challenges of life due to their lack of living out the principles? Also, many pastors know what it's like to labor intensively to teach sound doctrine and still witness some of their members fall prey to lies that will ultimately rob them of the what God has for them. Even where the truth is being taught there must also be a warning about how wolves can come in and devour the sheep. It is heartbreaking to see even one sheep fall by the wayside.

Finally, almost every pastor knows what it is like to cast a vision for a brighter, better future, only to have people within the congregation sow seeds of discord and do everything they can to undermine that God-given vision, all while not having any resources to waste at all. Being a pastor is a life calling that is inextricably bound to the outcomes of the people they serve. Again, that's what a shepherd is—a sheep herder.

So then, the desire to experience a feeling of effectiveness in ministry is often inescapable due to things that are completely out of a pastor's control. If people are excited and on board with the vision, then things move easier. But if they are not on board, or have been lured to some other alternative focus, things can be very hard. My point is simply this: in business and investing you get out what you put in. In ministry, that is not necessarily so. You can put all that you have into ministry and not see the return that you expect. Because after all, ministry is not about what you can get out of it, it's about giving back to God what He requires, which is faithfulness and trusting in Him enough to leave the results up to Him no matter what.

Thousands of pastors quit the ministry regularly and there seem to be very few people who are willing to talk about why. I have just shared with you a few of the reasons, and none of these were foreign to Pastor Derek Washington, Senior Pastor of Greater Pleasant M.B. Church.

Ministry is not about what you can get out of it, it's about giving back to God what He requires, which is faithfulness and trusting in Him enough to leave the results up to Him no matter what.

PASTOR DEREK

Derek was in a place in his ministry where he was feeling like giving up. But it wasn't always bad for Derek. He was involved in a history-shifting event in his hometown of Driscoll, NC, where he served as pastor. As a young community organizer, he worked tirelessly to fight against the misallocation of government funds that robbed poorer communities of their resources and sent those same resources to wealthier areas in the city. There were numerous documented cases of funding for schools, community halls, and workplace development centers that somehow never seemed to make it to the designated neighborhoods. All the while the paper trail would lead to new parks, bike trails, and zen gardens in areas of the city that were already developed and flourishing. Pastor Derek's zeal, dedication, and also his success at taking on city hall with a cadre of lawyers and activists led him to have a lot of credibility within the community where he would later serve as pastor. This type of community involvement from clergy is the kind of action that people needed to see to be open to hearing the message that he preached. He had more than just blind optimism, he absolutely felt endowed by God to do a work in his community.

He went through the process for ordination, matriculated through a highly respected seminary, and submitted to his leadership along his path of ministry to help him fully develop. He well understood that ministry would get very hard at times. He was no stranger to fighting. He had fought many battles and won. But as time progressed, he began to feel as though there were only so many battles he could fight. His wife Vanessa and his children did all they could to support him, but they rarely knew the intensity of the battles he faced. He veiled much of the challenges as to not taint their hearts toward ministry and the congregation. It's hard to hug and greet someone who has stabbed your dad in the back, so Derek held in a lot of secrets. Resignation is a Hazardous Attitude that says, "What's the use?" Derek was feeling the effects of it big time. The only question is, how would he respond?

IT'S AN EMERGENCY

It was one of those Saturdays that started so good that something had to go wrong. It was the kind of day that even though you couldn't quite put your finger on why, you were bracing yourself for the inevitable. Pastor Derek Washington arrived at his church for a meeting with the

Finance Committee. As he exited his vehicle he saw Sarah, one of the Finance Committee members who was also the wife of the chairman of his deacon board. Just as he placed his vehicle in park, she lowered her phone from her cheek, revealing tears.

"Pastor Derek, it's an emergency. Marshall's had a massive heart attack and he's been taken to Veterans Memorial," Sarah notified Pastor Derek.

"Oh no, let's go to the hospital right now," Pastor Derek replied to Sarah.

"Yes, Elizabeth is going to take me right now," Sarah advised.

"I'm right behind you. Don't worry. I'll be praying." The reason Pastor Derek told Sarah not to worry is because worrying would not help in a situation like this; it wasn't because she had nothing to worry about.

You see, Sarah's husband Marshall and Pastor Derek had become great friends over the years. Not acquaintances or just good church members, I mean real friends. Marshall was a genuine person who was honest, dependable, and loyal. All the characteristics you would want in a friend, all the qualities any pastor would want in a deacon serving at their church. So, the truth was that Pastor Derek himself was worried. He was worried for Sarah and the children, he was worried for his friend Marshall, and he was even worried about what Marshall's absence might do to the church.

As they entered the emergency room parking lot there was a single ambulance with the lights running and the back doors were open. With an uncanny synchronized precision, Sarah, Pastor Derek, and Elizabeth all jumped out of their vehicles in unison and entered the ER. There standing in the doorway was the attending physician who ushered them into a consultation room. The door shut in a way that seemed to announce finality. As his long white coat draped down his body, the doctor placed his hands on his knees and slowly lowered himself into his seat while simultaneously exhaling for what seemed like an eternity. And then he began, "Marshall has suffered what is most commonly referred to as widow maker and unfortunately, he has lost a portion of the function of his brain. The good news is that he could still recover, but I want to be honest with you when I say he has the deck stacked against him. Do you have any questions?" the attending physician surmised.

After his assessment, Sarah belted and wailed in a deeply sorrowful way. She hadn't lost hope, but she loved Marshall immensely and did not want to see him go through such a great challenge to his health. Elizabeth consoled her, while Pastor Derek peppered the doc with clarifying questions about his friend's newfound predicament. The situation was bleak, but they still had their faith. Derek wondered how he would ever do life and ministry without Marshall.

DID YOU GET MY EMAIL?

The next day at church, Pastor Derek was there but not really there, if you know what I mean. You could say he was at the church physically, but as far as his mind, he was mentally at the hospital with his friend. As far as his heart, emotionally he was with Sarah and the kids. But as far as his feet were concerned, he was back at the office, right back to serving the congregation, expected to be "all systems go", with little to no time to process what had happened the evening before. The dire situation with his friend and chairman was still unfolding. By now word had gotten around that Marshall had a serious heart attack with a less-than-optimal prognosis.

Though the members of Greater Pleasant were praying, there was still a communal sobriety for what might occur. Pastor Derek well understood that he needed to present a face to the congregation as though he was confident about his friend's healing, but the reality of the diagnosis was weighty. So, he would do everything he could to make Sunday morning as fruitful as possible. After all, though he, Sarah, and many of the other congregants were hurting, they were still a church. And people were still coming through the door who needed to hear the good news. Pastor Derek had isolated himself to his study and had finished praying. He was a bit miffed that the deacons were not in the study to pray at the normal time. It felt lonelier than it should for obvious reasons. Marshall would normally be the one to round everyone up. Did it only take one day for their prayer time to fall apart? As Pastor Derek opened the door to his study to go out to the sanctuary, he was met by the Vice Chairmen of the Deacon Board. Surely this was someone who would share in his concern for his friend Marshall and understand his need for support to be able to walk out and uplift the congregation when he was really in need of some uplifting himself. But that's not exactly why Ross, the Vice Chairmen, was standing there in the hall waiting on him to finish the prayer that he should have been leading in Marshall's absence. Ross had a very concerned look on his face. He was clearly waiting to speak.

His eager posture made Pastor Derek interested in hearing what he had to say.

"Hey Pastor, did you get my email about the kids riding their bikes through the church parking lot?"

Pastor Derek stood petrified hoping something better would follow. The chairmen of the deacon board, and Pastor Derek's dear friend was fighting for his life, and the most urgent matter he brings to him, after missing prayer, is kids taking a shortcut through the church parking lot on their bicycles. Pastor Derek took a deep breath and then responded, "No Ross, I haven't gotten to your email yet considering." He ended his sentence with the word "considering" as if to lead Ross to the conclusion that given the current circumstances, no one cared about kids riding their bikes in the church parking lot.

Ross, totally missing the "considering que" decided to double down, "Well you've got to stay up on your email inbox, pastor, this is something that people care about and it needs to be addressed."

At this point, Pastor Derek is filled with regret that he ever ordained Ross and made him a leader in the church. But he did, so he must shepherd him too. He took a deep breath before he responded and said, "Ross thank you for letting me know. We'll address the matter in the next meeting." Truth be told, Pastor Derek is deeply annoyed that someone, anyone, especially a leader, could be so tone-deaf in discerning the times. Ross has a concern. Great. His concern isn't "how can I take on Marshall's duties," seeing as how he is Vice Chairmen. His concern isn't "how can we support the family in this very difficult time?" His concern isn't even to ask about Marshall's condition or if he is expected to pull through. This was the part of pastoring that Pastor Derek found deeply troubling but understood that it was sometimes par for the course. He secretly longed for committed, sincerely genuine people to occupy the leadership positions on the team. He often felt responsible when reality emerged to remind him that this was not always the case.

DAY-TO-DAY

What does a pastor even do every day? The day-to-day responsibilities of a pastor often include counseling members who find themselves needing direction and spiritual covering, mitigating and arbitrating marital and other family issues, and gaining knowledge and information concerning the next steps for major financial decisions that the church is considering. This includes navigating city, county, and even state politics at times while also circumventing the internal political wake.

On a day-to-day basis, a pastor often has to proofread messaging and communications sent to the congregation. Not for spellcheck purposes but for the concern of mission drift. Pastors are mission-minded, and they understand how confusing it can be when what is communicated to the group does not perfectly match what the group was told is the vision. There is also the never-ending pursuit of raising funds to keep the mission going due to the lack of financial support by some. All while dealing with scrutiny from the community on the church's budget allocations. Everyone feels they know what the church should spend money on, whether they give financial support or even attend a church at all. We can't forget the basic functions that are expected of every pastor such as performing weddings, funerals, pre-marital counseling, appearances at family events, and so forth and so on. There's the strain of noncommittal members and the endless brainstorming of how to spur them on to faithful engagement. But the most important thing pastors do is developing and writing sermon series to feed the sheep. It's a great challenge to not allow the other tasks to compete with the one that's most important. Many pastors have also been surveyed saying they feel lonely, have experienced a loss of close relationships, and that they experience a lack of genuine connection with other pastors who share the same burden. But one of the hardest things that pastors face is betrayal, having someone whose feet have been under their dinner table show acts of malice toward them, dining and socializing in close proximity with the intent to undermine the work that the church is doing the entire time. There's this feeling that though the pastor sees the work of the church as serious as life or death, some people seem to respond as though they could take it or leave it. This was discouraging but it never stopped Pastor Derek from living out the mission himself. He engaged whomever God placed in his path, like Dre, a kid from their neighborhood that Pastor Derek had been praying for, for a while.

"Yo Pastor Derek!" Dre shouted.

"Hey Dre, good to see you man," Derek responded.

"I'm liking the new sound system the church has."

"Thanks, Dre, it was a big decision to purchase it but I think it was worth the investment."

"Pastor Derek, I could make it sound even better."

"Oh really? Why do you say that?"

"I used to be an engineer for a major record label before I moved to Durham to be closer to my son's mom. It's what I do. Have you heard of this youngster who's number one right now, Kid Money?"

"Yes, how could I not know who Kid Money is? The youth department would vote me out if I didn't," Derek said jokingly but sorta seriously.

"Well, I mixed every single one of his records," Dre bragged.

"Wow man, you're big time! Sounds like we could definitely use your expertise."

"Thank you," Dre replied. "I'll be glad to come to your services and get it right."

As a pastor, Derek immediately picked up on Dre's choice of words. He said, "your services" and not "the services" or even "our services". Derek understood that Dre did not see himself as a part of the church but rather somehow separate from it. Derek decided to inquire more. "Hey Dre, let me ask you a question. Are you a part of any of the men's discipleship groups?"

"Nah, I know that you guys have those, but I've never checked them out."

Ouch. Dre's choice of words again confirmed to Pastor Derek what he feared initially. "You guys" again implies that the church and Dre are not one and the same and that he didn't see himself as a part of it. Derek decided to engage Dre more. "Hey man, offering your gift is awesome but we are interested in more than just how your skills could benefit the congregation. I want you to know that I deeply care for your spiritual well-being also bro," Derek affirmed.

"Thanks so much Pastor Derek. I really appreciate it. Hey, let me know if you want me to run your system for you."

As Dre departed Derek couldn't help but compare this interaction with so many others he had in the past. It's normally a struggle to get people to serve and participate, but even when there is a desire to serve, it's usually because they see the church as an outlet for them to operate in their gift. They treat it like a singing venue if they like to sing, or a theatre if they like to be on stage, and there isn't any real commitment to growth and change mission-wise. The church is just a convenient platform for them to do their thing. And while that may seem ok, if you get a house full of non-committal people that aren't invested, you've got a community center on your hands and not a church.

If you get a house full of non-committal people that aren't invested, you've got a community center on your hands and not a church.

Just two weeks later, Pastor Derek was the guest speaker at a church not too far from Greater Pleasant. He couldn't help but admire and appreciate the amazing media ministry the church had. As he prepared his heart and mind to preach, the sermonic solo began, and the singer's voice was crystal clear. The Hammond organ was permeating the body, soul, and spirit. Derek thought to himself, "Not only can this young lady sing, but this sound engineer is also working this house!" He did as many speakers might do; he looked to the middle of the room to see if he could see who was working the soundboard, and that's when it hit him. There behind the controls was Dre, working the soundboard and even wearing a church t-shirt for the technical ministry. The previous conversation he had with Dre began to involuntarily play in his mind. He began to pepper his own heart with questions such as, "Did I push him to be a part of discipleship too hard?" "Should I just let him work the soundboard if that's all he wanted to do?" "What does this church have that Greater Pleasant doesn't?"

Just when his mind was getting the best of him, he decided to put all of those self-doubting thoughts to rest. It was now time to preach. Despite all that was happening with his friend's health, tone-deaf leaders, and doubting his own leadership, he stood to preach and did a masterful job. No one noticed a thing. His heart was heavy but through prayer he nurtured his spirit to be light. After the service he was greeted by Dre. "Hey, Pastor Derek, did ya'll ever find someone to run your sound system?"

"Good to see you, Dre. No, not yet," Derek responded reluctantly.

"I might know somebody," Dre solicited. You may already understand why Dre's sudden desire to help fill the role was a bit off-putting. Derek had someone in mind also. That would be Dre.

"Thank you Dre. I appreciate your help. Please send me that name." Though Derek was willing to be open to Dre's suggestion, he also loathed the idea of starting over again with a new relationship. He wondered if this would be different at all from the last time.

THE JENKINS WANT TO MEET FOR LUNCH

The next morning Pastor Derek rose early and spent some time in prayer and reading his Bible. Visitation hours at the hospital started at 9 a.m. and he wanted to be there first thing in the morning to get an update on Marshall's progress. But before he could get out of the door, his wife Vanessa had a message for him. "Babe I talked to the Jenkins' last night; they want to meet for lunch." Vanessa prepped her husband, Derek.

"Okay, well, that's no problem right?" Derek pleaded for affirmation.

Vanessa replied without saying a word. She just gave Derek one of those looks that says *I know you're hoping for the best*, but it didn't sound like that kind of request. You see Derek and Vanessa understood what many pastors do, that people often want to go to lunch with the pastor when they want something from them, or they have bad news to share, and they respect them too much to send the news via text.

"Alright, I will call them on my way to the hospital," Derek resolved. Derek kissed his wife, Vanessa, hopped into his

Ford Focus sedan, and started on his way to Veterans Memorial Hospital.

As he got on the expressway, he began to survey in his mind all the different things they could possibly want to talk about over lunch. He went back and forth until he realized that if he was going to call them, he had better call now because he only had ten minutes left to drive. As the phone began to ring Derek was still wondering what it could be. Then he got an answer.

"Hello, Pastor how are you?" Bro. Jenkins greeted.

"I'm doing well, sir, how are you?" Derek asked.

"I can't complain one bit, can't complain one bit."

"Hey, listen, my wife said that you all wanted to meet for lunch, is there something you want to discuss?" Derek inquired.

"Well yes pastor, we would like to meet for lunch or we can just do this over the phone now, whichever works best for you."

In Derek's mind, this was not a good sign. He didn't feel at all that this was going to be a good phone call and the whole "do this over the phone" was jarring. Though Derek is sitting on the edge of his seat, he delays his response because he is preparing for the worst. But alas, the deafening silence had to end.

"Bro. Jenkins, sure thing, what's on your mind?" Derek asked.

"We are going to be leaving the church. We haven't felt included in the direction that you've been taking us in for quite some time. No hard feelings or anything, we are close to you guys, and we love you, but we feel it's time for us to go in another direction."

Derek was heartbroken. He loved the Jenkins dearly. They had been there for his entire tenure at Greater Pleasant and they were Godparents to his children. They would regularly babysit the kids so he and Vanessa could get away from the rigor and race of ministry. Thanksgiving was spent together every year in addition to a select few other families. The Jenkins were not just church acquaintances, they were family. The loss of this relationship would be saddening for Derek, Vanessa, and their children. Finally, deciding that the air of silence had reached an unbearably uncomfortable length, Derek responded to Bro. Jenkins.

"Can you tell me what it is exactly? Why is it that you guys feel you need to leave? We love you, and you're family to us. I hope that's what we are to you." Derek felt as though he had given a good, heart-felt response. He wasn't, however, prepared for the response that he would receive in return.

"We don't believe in your vision anymore. I am so sorry to say that, but we don't. Last year when the children's building was opened to the neighborhood kids it changed the landscape of our church and we feel it should be for our children first and foremost."

Just like that Derek realized what this was all about. Greater Pleasant had a children's ministry building that was more than adequate to house the various programs and activities that they were running for the youth. The building was highly underutilized. So, to steward such a great resource as best as possible, they decided to open the activities and programs to any child in the community, whether they were a member or not. Whether they had a grandparent there or not. Turns out there was a small contingency in the church that did not agree with this "come one come all" philosophy of ministry. What Derek could not believe was that the Jenkins were a part of it. This is another peril of pastoring. On the one hand, these members paid for the building with their offerings, and they did not do so thinking that their kids may not always have priority in the facility. There was also an increased security concern by being more open to anyone in the community; volunteers had to increase to man the space, and there was also a slight increase in utility expenses due to the building being open longer. Those were the facts, but Derek was focused on the truth. Eighty percent of the homes in the neighborhood were single-parent households and the church was called and equipped to help. This often left young boys and girls without supervision, instruction, or direction and the truth is that these are all things that the church should provide. So, while Pastor Derek was always very willing to hear the concerns of detractors, nothing prepared him for people deciding to leave the church because the church was being the church. The loss of close relationships is always difficult, but far too common for people in Derek's role. Derek wondered if his leadership had reached it's shelf life. It was now time to let that conversation rest and finally go inside the hospital to see his friend Marshall.

I THOUGHT WE WERE ON THE SAME TEAM?

When Pastor Derek arrived at Marshall's room, he was surprised to be greeted by Victor, another pastor in the same community as Greater Pleasant. Victor was the pastor of a large church and a real estate investor. Derek didn't know that he and Marshall knew each other, but he knew that the only way he was able to get to Marshall's room was because he was clergy due to the seriousness of Marshall's condition.

"Pastor Derek, how are you?" Victor greeted Derek.

"I've been well, Victor, it is good to see you. How's our friend?" Derek asked Victor.

"He's hangin' in there. He's a fighter," Victor assessed.

Needless to say, it was very difficult for Derek to witness his friend and church member lying lifeless on the hospital bed with tubes running almost everywhere through his body, but he couldn't quite put his finger on why Victor was there. Marshall wasn't able to respond at the moment so he couldn't do any harm. But Derek still wondered why Victor seemed to emerge at a time like this.

"Well, I'll be on my way. I was hoping he could talk but I'm glad I got to see him," Victor said to Derek.

"Okay, Victor. Take care," Derek responded.

As Derek sat by the bedside of his friend Marshall, he was filled with so many emotions. His mind began to think of so many things like the emotional well-being of Marshall's wife Sarah, his children, and the leadership void this would leave in the church if he didn't pull through. But there was one other pressing issue that consumed Derek's thoughts. Greater Pleasant had seen better days financially and Marshall was a key person in helping them get out of the hole they were in, specifically their mortgage. Greater Pleasant had grown exponentially over the course of just a few years, and they began to build additional spaces on their property off of forecasted growth. The problem was that to build the additional space, they took on additional debt. First was the line of credit they borrowed against the equity in their property. Second was the entirely new construction loan, not forgetting that the original mortgage had not been paid off, either. This combined with a sudden decline in attendance due to two prominent families no longer seeing eye to eye created the perfect storm for the financial well-being of the church.

When Derek became pastor, two large families did the majority share of the serving and the giving, both of which had family members as associate ministers at Greater Pleasant. When neither became Senior Pastor, they began to become disgruntled and made sure that other people were unhappy as well. One minister took his family and many of the members in one direction and started his own church, and the other minister took his family and another large group of members in the opposite direction and started his own church. Derek was left with all the debt and real estate of a once thriving megachurch now splintered in three different directions. Marshall was such a unifier and he had been there longer than Derek. He was able to get families to sit down and talk to each other even though they disagreed on the direction of the church. He was also the chair of the finance committee as the chairman of the deacon board. Marshall took special responsibility for working to get the budget balanced and to get buy-in for the various high-capacity givers to contribute, but all of this was just getting started. The present reality was that Greater Pleasant was in trouble and the bank was calling.

It wasn't until three weeks later that Derek learned why Victor was at the hospital that day. Derek finally decided that he could not kick the can down the road any longer as it related to dealing with the bank. Greater Pleasant was now sixty days behind on their various mortgages. As Derek waited in the seating area to talk to the president of the bank, he saw him wrap up his previous meeting. There, peering through the window, Derek witnessed a gentleman dressed really sharp, like a preacher, shaking hands with the president of the bank, and then putting on his topcoat and hat. Derek recognized the man's body language and mannerisms but when he turned around to exit the door it confirmed Derek's suspicions—it was Victor. Victor looked at Derek, he didn't really acknowledge him or say hello, but instead offered a sheepish grin and exited the building. Derek was allowing his imagination to run wild, only to be interrupted by the president calling for him to enter.

As they both were seated, the silence was broken by a very long sigh by both Derek and the president of the bank. The president spoke first. "Pastor Derek, things like this are never easy, but as you know, Greater Pleasant is severely delinquent, and we just received a strong offer for your property." Now Derek was normally a calm person, but he was now furious. If you're wondering which part of the president's sentence made him so angry, the "delinquent" part, or the "we now have a strong offer" part, it would be the strong offer part that angered Derek. He knew with every fiber of his being that Victor, hearing the church was in trouble, went to cut a deal with the bank. Pastor Derek was absolutely correct. Another pastor, who was presumably on the same team, went to the bank to guarantee the purchase of Greater Pleasant's real estate if they foreclosed. What Victor had done was the lowest of the low, not to mention showing up at Marshall's intensive care unit room and being disappointed because he couldn't "talk".

Derek thought to himself, *how could another pastor do this to me*? How could someone who was supposed to be on the same team as me do something so horrific? As a real estate investor, Victor understood that the one reason banks are hesitant to foreclose on a church is because the property can only be used by another church, and that makes re-sale difficult. So, Victor took care of that by offering his own church as a buyer. If pastors sometimes die a death of 1,000 cuts, this was a gash. Derek decided to respond to the bank president the best he knew how. "Well, sir, hopefully, it won't come to that. We are going to do everything in our power to get caught up as soon as possible." With that, Pastor Derek exited the office and departed in his vehicle. It didn't sound like a lot, but it was all he had to give the bank president as assurance that Greater Pleasant would not default on its financial obligations. As Derek drove down the street, putting the bank in his rear-view mirror, he wondered if ministry belonged there also. But there was no time to allow those thoughts to fester. Pastor Derek was headed home to eat dinner and change clothes. He had to get ready for their church business meeting.

ROBERTS RULES OF ORDER

Pastor Derek decided to leave his house early. There was so much that had transpired that day—and that entire week for that matter—and he wanted to settle his heart and mind and not drag any of that into the church business meeting. He felt as though he needed at least one thing to go well that week. To his surprise, when he arrived at the church parking lot it was already full. He thought to himself, "Did someone change the meeting time?" As he exited his Ford Focus, he saw two of his trustees standing at the door waiting for him. To Derek, this was not a good sign. He felt that if it was anything good, then he would have known about it.

As Pastor Derek approached the door, the two trustees looked at each other as if they were both trying to decide who would actually speak. Finally, the one on the left spoke up, "Hey Pastor Derek, tonight may not go well." That was exactly what Derek was hoping for, that it would go well. At least now he knew he could hope for something else.

"What do you mean it may not go well?" Derek inquired.

To that the trustee on the right responded, "They are waiting for you." The two of them then turned and walked into the meeting room. As Pastor Derek stood there and tried to gather his thoughts, he was floored at the greeting he received. Was that all the prep he would get for what he was about to walk into? Pastor Derek took his seat at the front table in the jam-packed room next to Ross, the Vice Chairman of the Deacon Board. Surely all of these people were not here to discuss kids riding their bikes through the church parking lot. Ross then called the meeting to order. As Derek scanned the meeting agenda, the first line item was the finance report. It was then that Derek knew his time was up. The finance report was always the last part of the meeting, not the first. Members had already gotten wind that someone—that would be Victor—had submitted a competitive offer for all of Greater Pleasant's real estate. Ross began, "Okay tonight we are here to . . ." and he was immediately interrupted.

"How could you let this happen, Pastor Derek?!" One member started.

"Why didn't you see this coming?" Another member questioned.

For the next forty-five minutes, Derek was peppered with questions about mortgage debt that was now delinquent, and none of which he created in his tenure as pastor. All the loans in question were originated before Derek was elected as the Senior Pastor of Greater Pleasant. Nevertheless, the loans became delinquent under his watch.

The meeting went on and on as more of a shouting match than a time of constructive discourse. Pastor Derek understood their anger and frustration and desired to do all that he could to bring some sort of solace. "This is a time for us to band together like never before. To be sure of our calling and mission like never before. It's a time for each of us to take a good assessment and examine our part. I'm asking each of you to give sacrificially to move the ministry from the red into the black. If each of us unite and come together, God will make it happen. He always blesses the unity of his people." Derek exhorted.

At this point, he wasn't sure if people were going to latch on to the message he shared or revolt even harder. In Derek's mind, he was either about to be voted out as Senior Pastor or just go ahead and resign. Either way, he began to daydream about what it would be like to go to bed that night without the burden of leading the church on his shoulders. It was at that moment that one of the members in the meeting spoke up. "He's right, you know. If we come together, we can do this and we can turn this thing around." There were a few freckled amens throughout the room.

Shortly after that, the meeting ended without voting on a new pastor, and without any more shouting. It was 8 p.m. and Derek had time to get back to the hospital to check on Marshall before the 9pm cut off.

TAKEN CARE OF

When Derek arrived at the hospital, he noticed Marshall's wife Sarah seated in a chair in the hallway, and the door to his hospital room was open. Sarah was seated just beyond the door entrance, so as Pastor Derek approached her, he could see into Marshall's room. As Derek peeked his head inside the room, it was startling to see the bed was neatly made with fresh clean sheets. He began to sob uncontrollably because he knew that Marshall was gone. Marshall died just a few hours before Derek had arrived, and Sarah had already begun to accept the harsh reality of his passing. "He's healed now. No more of the cares of this world. It's alright now. It's alright," Sarah comforted Derek.

"That's right," Derek affirmed. "I just didn't think we would be saying goodbye so soon."

The next two days were spent making all the final arrangements for Marshall and his Celebration of Life service. Pastor Derek found refuge in his purpose of serving the family in this regard. It was something he had done numerous times throughout his pastorate, and it allowed him to occupy his emotions with caring for his friends and family. Derek actually found joy in helping with the service program, negotiating fees with the funeral home, and picking out Marshall's final suit he would wear on the day he was buried. He loved his friend, and it was all he could do to honor him and send him off in style.

As the days passed by, Sarah got a visit from their financial advisor. He rang the doorbell unannounced but she was somehow not surprised. "Hello there. Come on in," Sarah greeted Mr. Raymond.

"Sarah, please allow me to extend my condolences to you and your family. Marshall was an amazing man, but simply gone too soon."

"I agree. I agree," Sarah affirmed.

"I wanted to go over everything with you. Is now a good time?" Mr. Raymond asked Sarah.

"Sure, absolutely," Sarah responded. Sarah knew that Marshall met with him regularly, but she never joined the meetings. So, she was somewhat shocked to learn what she would hear next.

"Sarah, you guys did very well. Here's how Marshall's planning ended up." Sarah saw a figure at the bottom of a sheet paper to the tune of 6.7 million dollars. Marshall had invested wisely, and they were not big spenders at all. Sarah was overjoyed and she wept tears of happiness. Her very next phone call may surprise you. She immediately called Pastor Derek and asked him how much the church was behind on their loans with the bank. Derek advised her that the amount was steep. $670,000. Sarah and Marshall always tithed 10 percent of their earnings to the church. Marshall had placed an end-of-life gift provision in his will for the church. Sarah and Marshall were the vessels God would use to set Greater Pleasant back on track. Pastor Derek was beyond exuberant to hear the news. He always had faith in Marshall and knew he could count on him. He just never considered Marshall coming through like this. This blessing was the shot in the arm Derek needed to keep going. It was a lighthouse of sorts to him in an otherwise dimly lit season of ministry. He began to evaluate things differently and address the areas of his ministry where Resignation had begun to creep on. Sure, he was still attending church meetings and he was still preaching on Sundays, but Pastor Derek had begun to pull back emotionally and relationally from his members. Discouragement caused him to pull back spiritually from God by spending less time in prayer and reading his Bible less. His lack of drive had caused him to stop his weekly date night with his wife as well. This amazing blessing was what he needed to snap back. It was a sign to him that God was with him and that, as he had promised, He would never leave him.

Resignation—"What's the use?"

Antidote—Say it out loud: "I CAN make a difference."

I might possibly be the only pilot who will tell you that they learned how to land an airplane over the phone. Yes, you read that correctly. After months and months of training, my landings were horrible. They were what I called basketball landings because every time I attempted to land, I bounced the airplane down the runway three or four times before it settled to the ground. I was so overcome with bewilderment and frustration until one day, I called an airline captain with more than 20,000 flight hours, FedEx Captain Frank Wallace, an African-American pilot. The wisdom he shared with me twenty years ago about landing an airplane is the theory I use for landing to this day. I'll summarize what Captain Wallace told me in four words, "All the way down." He told me that I needed to fly the airplane all the way down to the runway. In other words, a landing shouldn't just happen to the pilot's amazement; rather, it needs to be intentional. "Pick your spot," he said, and "control what happens all the way down and never give up on it." "It's always too soon to quit." What a lesson!

How many people do you know who landed somewhere in life as a result of circumstances that happened to them versus taking responsibility for the parts they could control? Trust me, as a flight instructor, if I fly with a student who is surprised we're on the ground, I'm not signing them off. Now please don't hear me say that people should never find themselves in a wonderful circumstance that they themselves did not create. I have had wonderful opportunities bestowed because I was in the right place at the right time. Furthermore, I would never assert that people shouldn't find themselves in a very bad predicament that was no fault of their own doing. But the Hazardous Attitude of Resignation tends to befall people who are always surprised. They don't intend to live in a mode of intentionality because, well, what's the use? People who have adopted a "what's the use" mindset do not see a path forward within themselves to change a given set of circumstances. In fact, if things do go well, they attribute it to good fortune. Let's look at some of the opportunities Pastor Derek had to fall into the trap of Resignation.

ATTITUDE ADJUSTMENTS

1) **Death is not meant to be a crisis of faith, but just a fact of life.**

   The situation was bleak, but they still had their faith. Derek wondered how he would ever do life and ministry without Marshall.

Even though death and sickness are as common as apple pie, it is remarkable how many people allow them to cause a crisis of faith. Every single person who has ever been born will one day die. What we really disagree with is when they die. We can't give in to Resignation when loved ones depart. It's the last thing they would want us to do.

2) **Great leaders take problems and turn them into champions.**

   "Hey Pastor, did you get my email about the kids riding their bikes through the church parking lot?"

Pastor Derek stood petrified hoping something better would follow. The chairmen of the deacon board, and Pastor Derek's dear friend was fighting for his life, and the most urgent matter he brings to him, after missing prayer, is kids taking a shortcut through the church parking lot on their bicycles.

If there is anything that can make you feel like a failure as a leader, it's putting a person in leadership before their time. It is also isolating for leaders when they feel as though they aren't surrounded by people who share the same passions as they do. Instead of giving in to Resignation, consider that even the hard relationships are meant to shape something in your leadership. Dennis Rodman was considered a troublemaker. But Phil Jackson took him and won championships. Great leaders don't resign at the sign of knuckleheads. They lead them where they are.

3) Preach to the parade.

"We are going to be leaving the church. We haven't felt included in the direction that you've been taking us in for quite some time. No hard feelings or anything, we are close to you guys, and we love

you, but we feel it's time for us to go in another direction."

I admit this is a tough one. The loss of close relationships is something that will never get easy. Here is some amazing advice I received. Every leader, whether a preacher or not, must learn to "preach to the parade." This means that as a leader, you will constantly be saying hi and bye. It's just a part of any sizeable organization. People will come and people will go. If you accept that ahead of time, you'll be okay. If not, things will become very difficult. Preach to the parade and you'll be ok.

Instead of giving in to Resignation, consider that even the hard relationships are meant to shape something in your leadership.

Chapter 6

_____

THE TOOLBOX

SAY IT OUT LOUD

> "If you don't like something, change it. If you
> can't change it, change your attitude."
> —Maya Angelou

> "The greatest day in your life and mine is when
> we take total responsibility for our attitudes.
> That's the day we truly grow up."
> —John C. Maxwell

By now, after reading this far, my hope and dream for you is that something very important has happened. As you read the stories about Tony Decker, Eddie Esposito, Hailey Mitchell, Tharen Dylan, and Derek Washington, the easy part was seeing people you know. Relatives, co-workers, or present or previous bosses. Anyone you've met with a Hazardous Attitude likely jumped off the page. But to see the faults in other people isn't the purpose of this book at all. How is the word "e-n-e-m-y" spelled in your life? Is it really spelled "in-a-me?" The goal of each character's story is to demonstrate what a person with a Hazardous Attitude looks and feels like so that we can learn from their mistakes without paying for the lesson ourselves. As you've seen, each Hazardous Attitude has a corresponding antidote that needs to be spoken out loud:

THE FIVE HAZARDOUS ATTITUDES AND ANTIDOTES

1) **Anti-authority**—A person who does not want to be told what to do.
   Antidote—"Follow the rules. They're usually right."
2) **Invulnerability**—A person who believes that consequences won't happen to them.
   Antidote—"It could happen to me."
3) **Macho**—A person with an overinflated sense of self-ability.

Antidote—"Taking unnecessary risks is foolish."

4) Impulsivity—A person who acts before they think.

Antidote—"Not so fast. Think first."

5) Resignation—A person who feels they can't make a difference.

Antidote—"I can make a difference."

Scientists have proven that saying something out loud has two primary benefits. First, saying something out loud can help you envision the outcome you desire. This is seen in exercises where a person is asked to say the word "orange" repeatedly and then they are shown a purple square and asked what color it is, and the answer is usually orange. Why are they calling a purple square orange? Because what they said has caused them to envision it. Hailey Mitchell succumbed to the Hazardous Attitude of Macho. She didn't envision herself never making it to become a professional pilot. When her macho attitude surfaced, she should have said out loud, "Taking unnecessary risks is foolish" because our words can shape our outcomes. When Tony Decker repeatedly refused to perform the required check at his job that could have saved lives, he should have said out loud, "Follow the rules Tony, they're usually right." When Eddie Esposito was having close calls with his illegal operation, he should have said out loud, "It could happen to me." When Tharen Dylan acted impulsively and forged board member signatures, he should have said out loud, "Not so fast, think first." When Pastor Derek Washington felt like giving up, he should have said out loud, "I CAN make a difference."

The second reason saying something out loud can positively affect us is because saying something out loud can shape behavioral patterns. After all, this is what this is all about. We aren't applying the Attitude Adjustments in this book so we can merely feel or think differently. We want to behave differently so that we can have better outcomes. Remember, an attitude is a proclivity to respond to a given circumstance in a certain way. It's so much more than just a thought. It's a response. Thinking about robbing a bank won't land you in jail. Robbing a bank will. Shaping behavioral patterns with our words is easier than you might think. It's ingrained in us. It can cause a person to call a purple square orange. In fact, if a person says one thing out loud but does something else, it may be the sign of a bigger problem. It's very difficult to say one thing out loud while doing the opposite.

THREE WAYS TO MANAGE RISKS ASSOCIATED WITH HAZARDOUS ATTITUDES

1) Identify the Hazardous Attitude.

I have only met one person in my lifetime that had all five Hazardous Attitudes and I'm willing to bet he'll never pick up this book. So, by now you know exactly which one, or which ones, you have habitually fallen prey to in your life. Use your previous outcomes to call out the Hazardous Attitude. Remember, an attitude is a proclivity to respond in a certain way to a given circumstance. People who identify Hazardous Attitudes before they react can literally save their lives and the lives of others.

2) Measure the Risk

Measuring the risk involves taking an honest look at what you stand to lose if you give in to a Hazardous Attitude. What could you or the people under your leadership suffer? Measuring the risk is almost certain to cause us to reconsider.

3) Apply the Antidote

Once you have identified the risk and measured the risk, it's time to say the antidote out loud. Remember, it's very difficult to say one thing and do the opposite thing. Words shape worlds. Words shape our behavior patterns and help us envision the outcomes we desire.

PERSONAL MINIMUMS

Something every pilot must use, especially in their early days of learning to fly, is something called "personal minimums." Personal minimums are the absolute minimum or poorest conditions the pilot will fly in. If the conditions are outside of their personal minimums, they don't fly and instead stay grounded. Personal minimums for pilots include things like the lowest visibility they will fly in, the strongest wind speeds, and the lowest cloud cover. This may not mean much to you so let me explain. The standards of each pilot's own personal minimums are set BEFORE they are faced with the question of whether to take a flight, not DURING. Make sense now?

To every macho person, set your personal minimums for how you want to operate in life so that you know when you are operating outside of what is safe. To every impulsive person, remember, "If it's gotta be now, it's gotta be no." That's a good personal minimum to prevent you from making an irreversible impulsive decision. Or if you're an impulsive buyer, set a dollar amount you can spend without prior planning. If something is over that amount, it's an automatic no to prevent you from impulse purchases. To every person facing feelings of Resignation and feels like they can't make a difference, set a personal minimum on how long you will work without taking a vacation. I don't know about you, but I make my worst decisions when I am tired. Rest is an absolute must for a person battling Resignation. Personal minimums can save a pilot's life and I believe they can save you from you. If you set them ahead of time, you'll know when it's time to apply the antidote. And remember to say it out loud.

Words shape our behavior patterns and help us envision the outcomes we desire.

Chapter 7

THE APPEAL

WHY YOU CAN CHANGE YOUR ATTITUDE BUT NOT YOUR HEART

Before you go, I want you to know that this chapter may be the most important chapter in this book. However brief it may be, I believe this chapter contains more valuable information than all the other chapters combined. The previous chapters clearly illustrate Hazardous Attitudes and how they can cause great harm to those who allow them to go unchecked. Chapter 6 shares how you can effectively change your attitude and mitigate the risks associated with Hazardous Attitudes. But I couldn't end this book without telling you that though we can change our attitudes, there is a reason we cannot change our hearts, and the heart is where lasting change begins.

The word that the Bible most often uses for heart is the Hebrew word "leb." It is used to describe the innermost being of a person. It's where the passions and intuitions are. It's also where a person's drive is. Jeremiah 17:9-10 (NKJV) says: "The heart is deceitful above all things, and desperately wicked; Who can know it? I, the LORD, search the heart, I test the mind, even to give every man according to his ways, according to the fruit of his doings."

Has your heart ever deceived you? How many times could I count the ways! If you follow your heart, your desires, and your intuitions, you may be living a life of deception while following a faulty mechanism, the heart. My heart has deceived me over and over again, and I am sure yours has also. One of my favorite verses in the Bible is Deuteronomy 30:6 (NLT) "The Lord your God will change your heart and the hearts of all your descendants, so that you will love him with all your heart and soul and so you may live!" That's my hope and prayer for all who read this book, that God would not only change your heart but the hearts of all who come after you to fully live!

Jesus, the Son of God, died on a cross in our place, on our behalf, because of our sins. By doing so He reconciled us to God the Father, making the gift of salvation and eternal life accessible to anyone who will believe. He also resurrected Jesus from the dead and He still lives today. If you would confess with your mouth and believe in your heart that Jesus is Lord and that God raised Him from the dead, you will be saved. To receive salvation and the gift of eternal life, it's as simple as "sorry," "thank you," and "please." Say it out loud: "Jesus, I am sorry for the sins I have committed, thank you for dying in my place on the cross; please be the Lord of my life all the days of my life. Amen."

FOLLOW
THE
LEADER

STAY CONNECTED

f facebook.com/TheArtofAvail   @theartofavail   ⩘ AVAIL

AVAIL
PODCAST

THE AVAIL PODCAST
HOSTED BY VIRGIL SIERRA

www.ingramcontent.com/pod-product-compliance
Lightning Source LLC
Chambersburg PA
CBHW070539090426
42735CB00013B/3021